Harvard Business Review

ON

TOP-LINE GROWTH

THE HARVARD BUSINESS REVIEW PAPERBACK SERIES

The series is designed to bring today's managers and professionals the fundamental information they need to stay competitive in a fast-moving world. From the preeminent thinkers whose work has defined an entire field to the rising stars who will redefine the way we think about business, here are the leading minds and landmark ideas that have established the *Harvard Business Review* as required reading for ambitious businesspeople in organizations around the globe.

Other books in the series:

Harvard Business Review Interviews with CEOs

Harvard Business Review on Advances in Strategy

Harvard Business Review on Appraising Employee Performance

Harvard Business Review on Becoming a High Performance Manager

Harvard Business Review on Brand Management

Harvard Business Review on Breakthrough Leadership

Harvard Business Review on Breakthrough Thinking

Harvard Business Review on Building Personal and Organizational Resilience

Harvard Business Review on Business and the Environment

Harvard Business Review on the Business Value of IT

Harvard Business Review on Change

Harvard Business Review on Compensation

Harvard Business Review on Corporate Ethics

Harvard Business Review on Corporate Governance

Harvard Business Review on Corporate Responsibility

Harvard Business Review on Corporate Strategy

Harvard Business Review on Crisis Management

Harvard Business Review on Culture and Change

Harvard Business Review on Customer Relationship Management

Other books in the series (continued):

Harvard Business Review on Strategies for Growth

Harvard Business Review on Teams That Succeed

Harvard Business Review on Turnarounds

Harvard Business Review on Work and Life Balance

Harvard Business Review

ON

TOP-LINE GROWTH

A HARVARD BUSINESS REVIEW PAPERBACK

The *Harvard Business Review* articles in this collection are available as
individual reprints. Discounts apply to quantity purchases. For information and ordering, please contact Customer Service, Harvard Business
School Publishing, Boston, MA 02163. Telephone: (617) 783-7500 or
(800) 988-0886, 8 A.M. to 6 P.M. Eastern Time, Monday through Friday.
Fax: (617) 783-7555, 24 hours a day. E-mail: custserv@hbsp.harvard.edu.

Library of Congress Cataloging-in-Publication Data
Harvard business review on top-line growth.
        p. cm. — (The Harvard business review paperback series)
    Includes index.
    ISBN 1-59139-969-6
    1. Corporations—Growth. 2. Strategic planning. 3. New
products—Management. 4. Industrial management. I. Series:
Harvard business review. II. Series.
    HD2746.H374   2005
    658.4′06—dc22   2005017059
                                                          CIP

*The paper used in this publication meets the minimum requirements of
the American National Standard for Information Sciences—Perma-
nence of Paper for Printed Library Materials, ANSI Z39.48–1992.*

Contents

Harvard Business Review

ON

TOP-LINE GROWTH

A Time for Growth

An Interview with Amgen CEO Kevin Sharer

PAUL HEMP

Executive Summary

FAST GROWTH IS A NICE PROBLEM to have—but a hard one to manage well. In this interview, Kevin Sharer, the CEO of biotech giant Amgen, talks about the special challenges leaders face when their companies are on a roll. Sharer, who was also head of marketing at pre-WorldCom MCI and a division head and a staff assistant to Jack Welch at GE, offers insights drawn from his own experience—and from his own self-proclaimed blunders:

"I learned the hard way that you need to become credible and enlist support inside the company before you start trying to be a change agent. If you think you're going to make change happen simply by force of personality or position or intellect, you'd better think again."

And change there was: Under Sharer's leadership, Amgen overhauled its management team, altered its culture, and launched a couple of blockbuster products.

How do chief executives survive in that kind of dizzying environment?

"A CEO must always be switching between different altitudes—tasks of different levels of abstraction and specificity," Sharer says. "You might need to spend time working on a redesign of your organizational structure and then quickly switch to drafting a memo to all employees aimed at reinforcing one of the company's values."

Having a supportive and capable top team is also key: "A top management team is the most revealing window into a CEO's style, values, and aspirations. . . . If you don't have the right top team, you won't have the right tiers below them. [The] A players won't work for B players. Maybe with a company like GE, the reputation of the company is so strong that it can attract top people to work for weaker managers. In a new company like Amgen, that won't happen."

Kevin Sharer knows something about growth. After stints as an officer in the U.S. Navy's nuclear submarine program and as a junior consultant at McKinsey, the Annapolis graduate went to work for General Electric in 1984. There, he served as a staff assistant to Jack Welch and later as general manager of two divisions, first software and then satellites, both in fast-growing and rapidly changing industries. He joined MCI in 1989 as head of sales and marketing, rising to president of the business markets division during a period of spiraling growth at the upstart long-distance provider. In 1992, he came to Amgen as president, chief operating officer, and heir apparent to CEO Gordon Binder. He became CEO in May 2000, when Binder retired, and chairman in January 2001.

Amgen grew to be the world's largest biotechnology company based on the success of just two products, both developed in the late 1980s: Epogen (an anti-anemia drug for kidney dialysis patients) and Neupogen (an anti-infection drug for cancer chemotherapy patients). Sharer's aim as CEO has been to broaden the company's offerings. One move has been the expansion into "small molecule" products, traditional chemical-based pharmaceuticals that can be formulated as pills. (Biotechnology's "large molecule" products are proteins that must be injected.) Sharer also has worked to boost the output of the company's R&D labs. Although the only new products to hit the market since Sharer became CEO are Aranesp (a second-generation anti-anemia drug that lasts longer between injections than Epogen) and Neulasta (a second-generation anti-infection drug with similar benefits over Neupogen), both have been big successes. Finally, Sharer has formed alliances with other biotech firms and gone on an acquisition campaign. The most significant acquisition has been Amgen's $11 billion purchase in 2002 of Immunex, the third-largest biotech company and the maker of Enbrel, a drug used to treat inflammation in arthritis patients.

These moves have spurred impressive growth. Revenue this year is expected to be around $10 billion, up from about $3 billion four years ago. Earnings could hit $3 billion, up from $1 billion. The market has at times been cautious in rewarding this growth, reflecting concerns about the company's product pipeline, Medicare reimbursement for its products, and challenges to its patents. But it's been a heady ride so far.

With the launch of its new products, Amgen has faced serious competition for the first time. Years ago, the company sold to Johnson & Johnson the exclusive rights to market Epogen (under the J&J brands Procrit and Eprex) *for nondialysis-related uses, including the anti-anemia treatment of chemotherapy patients. But because of a favorable legal ruling, Amgen has been able to enter this lucrative field with its new anemia drug, Aranesp, precipitating a fierce battle with J&J. In addition, Enbrel, the product that Amgen acquired when it bought Immunex, goes head-to-head against anti-inflammation products made by, among others, Johnson & Johnson.*

Competition requires the company to adopt a new mind-set, Sharer says. His office at company headquarters in Thousand Oaks, California, is decorated with paintings from his personal collection—some of them aggressive enough that colleagues have asked that they be removed from public areas. For example, a menacing work by British artist Ray Richardson depicts an unsavory-looking character pointing out of the frame to something—someone?—lying on the ground. Centrally positioned is a portrait of General Custer. It's a reminder, explains Sharer, that "you'd better not underestimate your competitors. You might lose everything." Next to it, though, is a portrait of Custer's Native-American scout with a different message—that "a leader's actions can have a devastating effect on others."

In this edited conversation with HBR senior editor Paul Hemp, Sharer talks in depth about how a "leader's actions" must be tailored to meet the demands of a high-growth environment.

What was your most unexpected lesson in leading for growth?

It was probably something I learned before I came to Amgen, way back in 1989, when I left GE and joined MCI as head of sales and marketing. It was a period of

extremely rapid growth at MCI. Although I had no back-
ground in the industry, I was pretty cocky. I remember
thinking, "Boy, they're getting one of GE's youngest VPs.
Aren't they lucky?" And within three months I went to
the CEO, Bert Roberts, and announced that we had the
wrong conceptualization of the business. Among other
things, I told him that we should be organized by markets rather than by geography. Ultimately, my ideas were
for the most part accepted and implemented. But that
didn't matter. The way I went about making my views
known guaranteed I was immediately isolated.

At GE, a new senior manager was expected to make
quick and dramatic change aimed at strengthening the
business, and I came into MCI with that ethos. Well, you
could do that at GE, but as a newcomer to MCI, this was
exactly the wrong approach.

The division presidents, whom I relied on to carry out
my sales and marketing initiatives, saw me as an adver-
sary who was trying to reorganize their jobs rather than as
an ally trying to win the brutal fight against AT&T. The
very people I needed felt I wasn't working in their personal
best interests—which was true, in a way. I was working in
what I thought were the best interests of the company.
But I was doing the right thing in the wrong way.

It took me nearly a year to figure this out. Finally, Bert
Roberts called me into his office and said, "Look, Kevin,
I've heard from a lot of the division presidents, and
you've got real problems. You've got to quit trying to do
their jobs." This stern warning really surprised me. But I
was lucky to get it. The pre-WorldCom MCI was like a
motorcycle gang out to do just one thing—get AT&T.
That's how tough we needed to be if we were going to
bring down a giant. When the gang members got nasty
toward one another, though, there was bound to be col-
lateral damage!

So I learned the hard way that you need to become credible and enlist support inside the company before you start trying to be a change agent. If you think you're going to make change happen simply by force of personality or position or intellect, you'd better think again.

So what did you do differently when you joined Amgen as president and heir apparent? Again, you were an outsider—and a somewhat unlikely one at that.

Right, here I was, this guy from the telephone business. The *Wall Street Journal* compared my arrival to John Sculley's arrival at Apple. Hiring me was definitely an out-of-the-box move by CEO Gordon Binder. He was a former CFO in a company of scientists, and I think he felt he needed a deputy who shared his business orientation. He knew that I probably could help out in sales, marketing, manufacturing, and engineering. And I guess he figured that if he'd hired the wrong guy, he'd know it in two or three years and could fire me, leaving enough time to find another successor.

Amgen was already tremendously successful when I got here in 1992. There were about 2,000 people, sales were a little over $1 billion, and the company was the leader in an industry—about which I knew nothing. My last brush with health care was ninth-grade biology.

So I set out to learn the business from the ground up—and to show my desire to learn. I listened in executive meetings. I made calls with sales representatives. I asked one of our scientists—a midlevel researcher named Gene Medlock, who was about my age and an easy guy to like—to teach me biology. He gave me reading assignments, and we'd have regular sessions in his office in front of a blackboard. Seven years later, as I was preparing to become CEO, I took six months and devoted roughly half my time to furthering my knowledge: I spent time in our labs, got tutored by a PhD biologist from McKinsey, and visited research chiefs at several pharmaceutical and biotechnology companies.

If I hadn't had that chastening experience at MCI, I could easily have blown up early on at Amgen. As it was, I became an insider before I started to make changes. And so by the time I became CEO, I'd already made enough changes that some people said it looked like a takeover from the inside. And it kind of was.

While yours was a fairly natural ascension to the CEO position, you have since shaken up the company in significant ways. Surely not everyone has been happy with this.

Yes, for Amgen to get to the next stage of growth, we needed to overcome some ingrained perceptions. Our first two products, Epogen and Neupogen, had been enormously successful. This led some people at Amgen to conclude that marketing isn't necessary if you have great products. Indeed, some viewed marketing as a threat to our science-based research and product development. "Science will provide" was kind of a mantra. Related to this was the belief that, because we had such great science, there wasn't much outside the company that we could benefit from.

But marketing *was* important. Even if we produced the greatest drugs in the world, we'd be in trouble if we couldn't get doctors to prescribe them or insurers to pay for them. As for our reluctance to look outside the company for ideas, I like to say that 0.1% of the biologists in the world work at Amgen. Those other 99.9% care about disease just as much as we do and are generating ideas that we should be aggressively looking at. There was another problem. When our only two products were Epogen and Neupogen, we had operated as a de facto monopoly. As we launched new drugs, we began to feel for the first time the heat of competition from the likes of Johnson & Johnson and Abbott Labs. So some changes had to be made.

Still, I didn't come to these conclusions in a vacuum. When it was announced in December 1999 that I was going to become CEO the following year, I asked the top 150 people in the company to meet with me for an hour each—150 hours in total. And I gave each of them the same five questions, which they received in advance: What three things do you want to change? What three things do you want to keep? What are you most worried I might do? What do you want me to do? Is there anything else you want to talk about? And I just listened for an hour. Many of the people came in with stuff written down, and in the case of those who didn't, I took notes. And then I tabulated all the responses, coming up with a pretty accurate and timely picture of what the top 150 leaders in the company wanted to do. I put all of this together and sent out a memo to the entire company summarizing my findings. These interviews gave me the mandate to do what I needed to do. It created a shared reality for the company and allowed people to begin aligning around a number of goals. The exercise was probably the single most important thing I did upon becoming CEO.

What's happened since?

Even in this short time, we've been through three or four different stages of growth. The first involved restructur-

ing the management team and changing the culture so
we'd be able to launch new products. Next, we took
action by acquiring Immunex and its popular drug,
Enbrel, and by launching Aranesp and Neulasta. Then we
entered a period of what you could call hypergrowth, as
we ramped up the production and marketing of those
three drugs, hired a lot of people, and expanded geo-
graphically. We were barely in control as we tried to keep
up with the growth. We almost went off the rails last year
because our accounts payable system was mainly paper
based. Today, although we still expect growth on the
order of 20% this year, we're more in control. It's a period
of consolidation.

Just this morning, I was talking with a division head
about how to get one part of the division to the next
level. Now that we've got all the organizational boxes
filled with people, we talked about whether the group has
the right structure and the right executive skills to support a company 50% bigger than we are now. Last year, I
wouldn't have had the time to have that discussion.

*Leadership isn't easy in this kind of dizzying environ-
ment. What has your approach been?*

Well, for one thing, a CEO must always be switching
between what I call different altitudes—tasks of different
levels of abstraction and specificity. At the highest altitude, you're asking the big questions: What are the company's mission and strategy? Do people understand and
believe in these aims? Are decisions consistent with
them? At the lowest altitude, you're looking at on-the-
ground operations: Did we make that sale? What was the
yield on the last lot in that factory? How many days of
inventory do we have for a particular drug? And then
there's everything in between: How many chemists do we

need to hire this quarter? What should we pay for a small biotech company that has a promising new drug? Is our production capacity adequate to roll out a product in a new market?

You have to be working at all of these levels simultaneously, and that's not easy. Jack Welch was the master of rapidly shifting between levels or even engaging with several altitudes at once. I made plenty of presentations to him as a staff guy and as a general manager. If you had weeks to get ready and Jack had none, you could stay even with him for half an hour. Then you were going to start losing.

But most CEOs tend to gravitate toward the altitude where they are most comfortable. That's natural. Someone might choose to operate almost exclusively at the highest possible altitude: "I'm going to be responsible for the company's strategic vision." Another might choose to operate mainly at a lower altitude: "I'm going to pick the curtains in that hotel." Both altitudes are important. But most CEOs who get in trouble do so because they get stuck at a particular altitude.

What's your *preferred altitude?*

Well, I certainly have a tendency to get tied up in the nitty-gritty details of a problem. In the Navy's nuclear submarine program, and particularly with Admiral Rickover, whom I served under, the expectation was that a young officer knew everything. If there was some component problem in the ship, you were expected to know, right down to the circuit level, how it worked and why it wasn't working. You weren't expected to take the screwdriver and fix it, but you were supposed to have comprehensive knowledge of the system.

There's a problem, though, transferring this ingrained tendency I have to a business setting. When I go into what I call my submarine mode—when I go very, very deep into a problem—I tend to think I can solve it myself, ignoring the advice of experts and closing down debate. I've paid a price for this—for example, in forging ahead with a product that others were telling me didn't have sufficient commercial promise.

There are other dangers in spending too much time at a low altitude. Regular, detailed operating reviews of major business units encourage financial discipline and accountability. But you have to be sure that you don't schedule these meetings too frequently and end up interfering with the very people you're trying to help. If you're not really careful, you can create a situation where people are doing nothing but getting ready for the next briefing.

Mainly, though, I prefer to work at a middle-to-high altitude. I'm fascinated with long-term strategic alternatives. I'm not a daydreamer, but because Amgen's financial resources give it a variety of options, I like to reflect on and talk about those options. Here, too, I sometimes have to force myself out of my comfort zone. I've decided that I need to look at these big-picture options two or three times a year and then put them away, unless a dramatic event changes the landscape. Otherwise, it can be destabilizing to the organization. People begin wondering, "What idea is Kevin going to have next?" I also have learned to be careful about ruminating on these things with the wrong audience. When you reflect on strategy, you're reflecting on the possibility of change, which can be unsettling if it seems to be always on the CEO's mind. So increasingly, I confine these discussions to a relatively small group of people.

Describe a day in which you had to make rapid shifts in altitude.

The day before yesterday, we had a morning executive committee meeting—our biweekly gathering of our top ten executives—in which we considered a range of issues. Do we make a $100 million investment that would involve dramatic changes in our European operations? This was a high-altitude kind of decision. We also did a country-by-country review of our biggest product. Which accounts are we winning and why? What does the sales force distribution look like? How did last week's revenue data point compare to the trend line? Down-on-the-ground sort of stuff.

Later in the day, I met with a consultant who is helping us do assessments of our executives. We talked about a CEO succession candidate who might take over six to nine years from now. The consultant had interviewed 20 people about this candidate, and he synthesized those discussions for me. So that's another pretty high-altitude activity.

And then I spent some time on, well, the shape of the boardroom table. Because our boardroom is too big, we can't get the kind of intimacy that I want. So I had the architects put together a mock-up boardroom table in another room that was a lot smaller. I wanted to see if we could get a shirtsleeves-rolled-up, around-the-kitchen-table feel. And I'm down in this room trying to decide how the dynamics of the group might change in that setting.

So you're always aware of the level you're working at and ready to move to another one?

Yes, but you also have to choose which of three broad areas you will focus on at any given moment: one, context—that is, the mission, aspirations, values, and leadership behavior that define a company—two, strategy, and three, execution. Obviously, a variety of altitudes exist within each of these three areas. Moving nimbly in and out of these areas and at different altitudes in each is crucial to leadership success, particularly in times of rapid growth and uncertainty.

So, for example, you might need to spend time working on a redesign of your organizational structure—a high-level, operational task—and then quickly switch to drafting a memo to all employees aimed at reinforcing one of the company's values—a low-level, context-setting task. Thinking of my job in this way helps me decide where to devote my energies and keeps me from getting stuck at one altitude or in one area. It also helps to ensure that the urgent doesn't crowd out the important.

In what ways can the urgent crowd out the important?

Actually, the urgent often *is* the most important. But it's easy to forget about other important items that aren't making immediate demands on you. For instance, it's easy to forget the importance of regularly educating the board about where the company is and where it's heading. It's critical that the management and the board stay in sync. And this is hard to do, because we're living this thing every day, whereas the board shows up four to six times a year for five to six hours. It's tempting to go to the board meeting and say, "Here are the results, here's how we're doing against budget, here's . . . here's . . . here's . . . Any questions? Thanks a lot."

But it's crucial that the board is thinking with you, particularly when you're growing fast. Because if you don't have the board with you, you can't seize opportunities as they come up. Yesterday we got fast approval for an acquisition because the board immediately understood where the company was and how this acquisition fit into our strategic and operational framework.

To take a more specific instance, in that discussion I had earlier this morning with the division head, we talked about the org chart for part of that function. It had too many cumbersome layers, in part because we're trying to accommodate some people by letting them keep their current positions. So the "urgent" is: How do we accommodate these people who, at the moment, we can't really afford to lose? The "important" is: How do we ultimately get the right organization in place? You might conclude that, because we have an urgent need to retain these people, we'll have to settle for a subpar structure. At the same time, we don't want the preferences of a few people to keep us from building a structure that will allow us to grow. In the end, we found a way—or at least I think we did—to deal with the right now and still find a path to the future.

One aspect of Amgen's growth is its workforce. How have you integrated all of these new people into the company?

I read a George Will column once in which he mused on what it took to be an American, as compared with what it took to be a German or a Frenchman. He said he didn't know what it took to be a German or a Frenchman. But he knew that to be an American, you really only had to believe in the Constitution, the Declaration of Independence, and the Bill of Rights, and either speak English or be learning to speak English. If you buy into that, you're American. And I thought to myself, "Gee, at our growth rate—half our 13,000 employees are new in the last two years—we're a company of immigrants! So what does it take to be part of Amgen?" Well, you've got to believe in our corporate mission—to serve patients. You've got to believe in and act on our corporate aspiration—to be the best human therapeutics company. And you've got to believe in our set of corporate values, which range from competing intensely to respecting one another. If you really believe in these, you're part of Amgen.

In developing these principles—our mission, our aspiration, and our values—we've tried to reinforce a common culture that will keep the organization aligned as we grow. We settled on these principles after a lot of discussion. For example, our corporate aspiration wasn't arrived at immediately. We could have aspired to simply be the biggest biotech company, but that wasn't very inspiring nor, by the late 1990s, very challenging. So we settled on aspiring to be one of the top-ten companies in market capitalization in our industry. I was responsible for this aspiration—and what a dud it was! During those interviews I had with the company's 150 most-senior executives, people basically said, "Top-ten market capitalization as an aspiration? You've got to be kidding. That sounds like GE or something. We're patient focused and science based. Why aren't we aiming as high as we can possibly aim? Why aren't we trying to be the best human therapeutics company in the world?" And that's what we adopted as our corporate aspiration.

All the new faces at Amgen include people at the top. Why have you brought in so many senior executives from outside?

A top management team is the most revealing window into a CEO's style, values, and aspirations. You can't overestimate its importance, particularly when you're growing fast—not to mention when you're migrating from a monopoly position to a competitive one, as we have. When you go from being a $3 billion company to a $10 billion company in four years, you'd better have people with $20 billion worth of capability in them. At this rate of growth, you want to overman the challenges, instead of always trying to play catch-up, because otherwise things will implode.

Not everybody can or wants to grow in capability and contribution at the same rate as the company. So how do you deal with somebody who at the $1 billion level is terrific and who at the $5 billion level is struggling in that same job? Sometimes you reduce the scope or complexity of the job. Sometimes you just say, "It's been a great ride, thanks a lot, we're going to help you get to a place that's more consistent with your abilities." Neither of those decisions is easy to make or implement. But they're necessary.

There's another problem: If you don't have the right top team, you won't have the right tiers below them. A-players won't work for B-players. Maybe with a company like GE, the reputation of the company is so strong that it can attract top people to work for weaker managers. In a new company like Amgen, that won't happen.

Of the ten-person executive committee, eight have been at the company for four years or less. I've been here for 12 years, and one fellow has been at Amgen for 21 years. His case is interesting. Dennis Fenton is the head of operations. Over the years, he's been willing to take jobs outside of his comfort zone. With no relevant experience whatsoever, he left manufacturing and took over sales and marketing for a while when the head of that division died suddenly. When I became CEO, he ran research and then human resources later on. Unlike some of his longtime colleagues, who found it hard to imagine a challenging and discontinuous future for Amgen, he had real fire in his gut.

How did you go about recruiting people for the top management team?

We had executive recruiters, but I also kept an eye out for people who might, for one reason or another, be open to changing jobs. We knew who we wanted as head of R&D, which was a new position with responsibilities that had formerly been the CEO's. This individual—Roger Perlmutter, an R&D executive at Merck—wouldn't return our phone calls, so we finally settled on another candidate we thought might work. One day, I noticed in the *Wall Street Journal* the announcement of a management change at Merck, one that looked like it might not be all that great for Perlmutter. So I asked David Baltimore, who's on our board of directors and a Nobel laureate, to call Roger, on the theory that scientists always return the phone calls of Nobel laureates. It worked. We got Roger to come out to the company and basically offered him a job that day. After some intense negotiation over the Christmas holidays, he joined us.

We also got our new sales and marketing head, George Morrow, by acting decisively. I had asked numerous people—consultants, financial analysts, doctors— whom they thought was the best sales and marketing manager in the industry, and his name came up time and again. I got an introduction to him through a mutual friend, and we had lunch. But he had a great job at Glaxo and was a possible candidate for the CEO job there. Then Glaxo and SmithKline announced plans to merge. My response? I showed up at his house in North Carolina on a stormy Friday night to try to sell him and his family on Amgen and California. After several months of discussion, we seemed close to a deal. And then he called to express some reservations about our proposed agreement with him.

A key hire was slipping away. A rapid altitude change was required. I canceled all my appointments and got a detailed briefing from our HR people on the complex elements of an executive financial package so that I could persuasively address his concerns. I then took out a blank piece of paper and spent four hours crafting a personal, absolutely from-the-heart letter that conveyed how much he had impressed us. I acknowledged his concerns and described as clearly as I could the opportunity he had to help us transform the company. He accepted the job.

So you get a super team in place. How do you ensure that you have the team's support?

The key, I think, is something that's easy to say and hard to do: I trust them. That means I give people a lot of freedom and flexibility and authority. For example, we're considering a major scientific investment. The head of research went and talked with a key board member about concerns the board might have with the investment so that he would be ready to answer questions about it at the next meeting. I didn't have to tell him to do that. And he didn't have to ask me if it was OK to go talk to a board member. This kind of independence is possible because the team is so capable and because we have very tight alignment around our goals.

Trust also means that the executive committee manages as a council. We really work together as a leadership team rather than as a rubber stamp operation for me. My model as CEO is the prime ministerial one, where if you don't have the support of independent, strong, and knowledgeable cabinet members, you don't have a job. This is quite different from the presidential model, where you have a bunch of people in the cabinet whom you may not know that well and whom you choose to fire every now and then.

This view of the CEO role is reflected in how I am evaluated. Each year, the nine people who report to me deliver to the board a collective review of my performance. I'm not in the room when this report is presented. Then the directors call me in and talk to me. It isn't always the most comfortable exercise, but it's healthy for everybody. I want to be a role model for my team by acknowledging that, like everyone, I can benefit from coaching. In fact, one of the best ways to grow as a CEO is to listen to your executive team, which has a near-perfect understanding of your leadership balance sheet.

Growth usually is accompanied by some awkward stumbles. What sort of mistakes have you made as Amgen has grown?

We've had our share of failures. One was the launch of a product called Kineret. It's a product that is very helpful to some patients with rheumatoid arthritis, and it was clearly a scientific breakthrough. But as company president in the late 1990s—and this is an example of my going into "submarine mode"—I failed to listen to the marketplace and people who were objective. I essentially said, "Look, I am going to decide the revenue potential of this product, and that's it." Then we spent money based on that estimated revenue potential, causing us to lose millions of dollars—because the potential was nothing like what I was asserting.

The seeds of this mistake are instructive. For one thing, my decision represented a bet by me that some clinical data not yet available would show this drug to be more efficacious than it really was. What drove me to make this seriously bad decision? Amgen had not had a new product in almost ten years, and we were desperate to show that we could innovate and move into the treatment of diseases that were beyond those of our two successful products. When a company that is growing rapidly becomes concerned that it doesn't have the products needed to sustain that growth, it can get desperate. And the likelihood is that you're going to make some marginal investment decisions in the pursuit of growth.

Another failure was the development of a product called Leptin, which in the mid-1990s got a lot of attention because people saw it as a cure for obesity. Everybody heard about this fat mouse that got real skinny. Columnist Dave Barry said that if the drug worked, "I'd inject my eyeballs with it." There was scientific evidence that this thing was a real breakthrough, and I told the product development guys to invest as much they needed to explore the drug's potential. And even when the initial results weren't very positive, we just kept investing. Now you could say that this was an aggressive pursuit of science, which in part it was. You could also say that we needed to learn how to say stop.

With Kineret and Leptin alone, I was responsible for investing millions of dollars of shareholder money unwisely. Hopefully, there's some stuff I've done on the other side of the ledger that balances it out. And those projects haven't been a complete loss. We teach cases about these failures in our new executive leadership development course, a four-day program for the top 400 managers in the company.

You can't let past mistakes, and the fear of making more, paralyze you. In fact, I like to say that sometimes you have to be willing to bet your job if you're going to move an enterprise forward.

How often have you placed that bet?

At least three times. The first was when I fired most of the management team and hired this entirely new group of people I didn't know. Maybe these people weren't as good as I'd thought. Maybe they didn't have the passion to make Amgen as good as it could possibly be. Maybe they wouldn't be able to work together. Maybe they wouldn't hire good people to work for them. Any of those possibilities could have derailed us. But I hired from the outside not because I thought it was a great idea but because I thought it was a necessity, given how much our business was changing. I felt that the company would fail if I didn't get the right leadership. My hope was that the people I brought in would be so unquestionably superb that current employees wouldn't have any doubts about why the hires were made. I think that turned out to be the case.

The second time I bet my job was when we decided in 2001 to buy Immunex, just as we were in the process of launching our first two major products in many years: Aranesp and Neulasta. And not just launching them, but launching them into a competitive market and with a brand new team. Furthermore, the acquisition posed more than just the usual challenges of integration. There was also the challenge of quickly ramping up production of Immunex's popular drug Enbrel, which was becoming somewhat tarnished in the marketplace because the company hadn't been able to make the product fast enough to meet demand. The acquisition has so far proved to be a success.

My third bet was the decision to go head-to-head against J&J, which until then had been a collaborator of sorts because of our licensing Epogen to the company. Just before I became CEO, we were considering an alliance with J&J to jointly market Aranesp, our new anemia drug. I thought that might make good strategic sense and had discussions over the course of a year with Bill Weldon, then head of J&J's pharmaceutical business and now CEO. Granted, there were difficulties in figuring out how to share the revenue. And it would be hard to overcome the litigious, Hatfield-and-McCoy history between the two companies. But this was a real option, especially given Amgen's lack of experience operating in competitive markets.

Then, at a meeting in Paris of the company's operating executives, I informally polled people during a cocktail reception. Everyone was dead set against a deal with J&J. They didn't want to rest in the company's shadow. "Okay," I said, "that's it. We're going to compete against these guys"—the biggest, toughest player in the game, against its biggest product. If it hadn't worked out, I wouldn't be sitting here.

What in you has prompted this risk taking?

Jack Welch was centrally important to me as a CEO role model. As a young assistant to him, I observed him often and up close—and at a time when he was making his boldest moves to change GE. He was struggling, but he continued to move ahead. I remember a top management meeting where he said with utter conviction that

GE was to become the most competitive enterprise and the company with the highest market capitalization on earth. This was during IBM's zenith, and I remember sitting in the audience and thinking, "Gosh, this is a fanciful goal." But his conviction made the hair stand up on the back of my neck.

Anyway, once I was making a presentation to some senior GE executives about acquiring RCA, after leading the team that did the analysis. Jack went around the table and asked everybody what they thought. Larry Bossidy, who was vice chairman at the time, said, "Boy, Jack, we're going to have to send a lot of people home in Indiana." I remember that because RCA had a big TV factory in Indiana. And as Jack continued around the table, I just kind of blurted out, "I've analyzed 300 companies, this is the best company, we need to do this acquisition, and we have to move on it." My boss, the VP of corporate development, who I hadn't cleared any of this with, went, "Uhhh, what are you saying here?"

Well, after we acquired RCA, Jack called me up into his office and said, "Hey, Kevin, I want to tell you something. Remember that meeting? There were two guys in the room who thought what you said was right —me and you. You took the shot, you said what you thought, and guess what? You were right. Good job, kid." I'll never forget that. His vision and aspiration for GE emboldened me in that meeting, and it continues to inspire me today.

It's one thing to talk about bold moves when a company is growing like gangbusters. How do you lead as a company gets bigger and growth inevitably slows?

I think honesty plays a key role. You have to articulate a credible and achievable strategy for the company. We think we can maintain very strong growth over the next three to four years with our current products. Beyond that, who knows? You simply can't see that far ahead. Until the FDA approves a product, it's all speculation.

So I try to be optimistic but realistic. My aim is to underpromise and overdeliver. That's the best approach in dealing with analysts and investors. And it's the best approach, I think, with employees. Besides, our employees have something else to motivate them besides spectacular financial results—our mission of helping patients and our aspiration of being the best human therapeutics company in the world.

Originally published in July–August 2004
Reprint R0407D

Funding Growth in an Age of Austerity

GARY HAMEL AND GARY GETZ

Executive Summary

EVERYONE KNOWS THAT CORPORATE GROWTH—true growth, not just agglomeration—springs from innovation. And the common wisdom is that companies must spend lavishly on R&D if they are to innovate at all. But in these fiscally cautious times, where every line item of every budget in every company is under intense scrutiny, many organizations are doing just the opposite. They tighten their belts, subject nascent product-development programs to rigorous screening, and train R&D staffers to think in business terms so the researchers will be better able to decide whether an idea for a product or service is worth pursuing in the first place.

Such efficiency measures are commendable, say authors Gary Hamel and Gary Getz. But frugality is not a growth strategy, they point out, and, in truth, there is very little correlation between corporate performance and the amount spent on innovation. Companies like Southwest, Cemex, and Shell Chemicals have shown that businesses don't have to spend a fortune on R&D to reap the benefits of innovation.

To produce more growth per dollar invested, companies must produce more innovation per dollar invested. Hamel and Getz explain how businesses can dramatically improve their innovation yields. They offer these five imperatives: Increase the number of innovators among existing employees (whatever their job titles) by involving them in innovation processes and events. Focus on developing truly radical ideas—ones that change customers' expectations and behaviors and industry economics—not just incremental ideas. Look for innovation sources outside the organization, as well as inside. Increase the learning from small, low-risk experiments. And commit to long-term, consistent development efforts.

GROWTH—REAL GROWTH—depends on innovation. Oh sure, a big acquisition can inflate a company's top line, but it's hardly fair to call this growth; agglomeration would be a better word. Deal making of the sort that was used to jack up revenues at companies such as Tyco, Vivendi, HealthSouth, and DaimlerChrysler is unlikely to produce above-average growth for more than a few years at a time. Study a company that has delivered strong revenue growth over a decade or more, and you're likely to find evidence of world-class innovation. Maybe the company invented a new industry structure, like Microsoft did when it "de-verticalized" the computer industry. Maybe the firm pioneered a bold new business model, like Costco did with its upscale warehouse stores.

Or maybe it hatched a bountiful brood of sleek new products, like Nokia did. Put simply, innovation is the fuel for growth. When a company runs out of innovation, it runs out of growth.

And there's the rub. We live in an age of austerity. Every line of every budget in every company is under perpetual scrutiny. Innovation budgets are no exception. Increasingly, R&D units are required to negotiate their budgets directly with key operating divisions, in hopes of tying their research spending to real-world customer problems. Companies like IBM are sending their R&D professionals into the field to interact directly with customers. Organizations are subjecting nascent development programs to ever more rigorous screening with the goal of focusing their resources on a few big-win projects. Additionally, companies are training their R&D staffs to think in business terms so the researchers will be better able to decide whether an idea is worth pursuing in the first place.

These efficiency measures are commendable, but they don't go far enough. A company can't outgrow its competitors unless it can out-innovate them. And in these austere times, that is only going to happen if a company is capable of substantially raising the yield on its innovation investments. Achieving such a step function improvement requires more than just a bit of R&D belt tightening. It demands a fundamentally new way of thinking about innovation productivity, as well as a set of strategies that have the power to deliver a whole lot more bang for every innovation buck.

To dramatically improve innovation yields, companies must believe that innovation outputs (new processes, products, services, and business models) are less than perfectly correlated with innovation inputs (cash and talent). This assumption is more unorthodox than it first appears. When we recently asked more than 500 senior and midlevel managers in large U.S. companies to identify the biggest barriers to innovation in their respective organizations, the number one response was "short-term focus" followed by "lack of time and resources." In this view, innovation is highly dependent on investment, and it is senior management's presumed obsession with near-term earnings that most limits a company's innovation productivity. We think this view is wrong.

A careful analysis of hyperefficient innovators reveals five imperatives for dramatically boosting innovation efficiency, each of which can be encapsulated in a simple ratio:

- **Raise the ratio of innovators to the total number of employees.** The greater the percentage of employees who regard themselves as innovators, whatever their formal job descriptions may be, the greater the innovation yield.

- **Raise the ratio of radical innovation to incremental innovation.** The higher the proportion of truly radical ideas in a company's innovation pipeline, the higher the innovation payoff.

- **Raise the ratio of externally sourced innovation to internally sourced innovation.** The better a company is at harnessing ideas and energies from outsiders, the better its return on innovation investments.

- **Raise the ratio of learning over investment in innovation projects.** The more efficient a company is at exploring new opportunities, learning much while risking little, the more efficient its innovation efforts will be.

- **Raise the ratio of commitment over the number of key innovation priorities.** A firm that is deeply committed to a relatively small number of broad innovation goals, and consistent in that commitment over time, will multiply its innovation resources.

We've resisted the temptation to turn these ratios into detailed metrics. Seeking too much precision at this early stage will merely reduce your chances of discovering new and fruitful ways of improving these ratios. At this juncture, three things are important: that you understand the principles behind the ratios, that you establish a broad baseline for your company around each ratio, and that you commit to achieving something like an order of magnitude improvement along each of the five dimensions of innovation productivity.

In the pages that follow, we'll describe these ratios and offer specific tactics that companies can employ to increase them. It's important to note that while we found plenty of cases in which companies improved their innovation performance by consciously focusing on one or two of these productivity drivers, we found no single company that had worked methodically to raise its game along all five dimensions. This is good news for your business. Chances are your competitors aren't even looking for nonlinear improvements to innovation efficiency. So there's plenty of scope for your company to distinguish itself—if it masters the art of innovating on the cheap.

Free Your Innovators

Years ago, J M. Juran and W. Edwards Deming showed that companies can reap big rewards by investing in the problem-solving skills of rank-and-file employees. Why, then, do so few companies invest in employees' capacity to innovate? While everyone may be responsible for efficiency and quality, senior management still views innovation as the province of specialized departments (R&D and product development) or the unexpected benefaction of a few dreamers. While most companies no longer squander their employees' intellect, many still waste a substantial share of their employees' imagination. The cheapest way to get more ideas into the innovation pipeline is to ask for them. Cemex, the highly inventive Mexican cement maker, devotes nine days each year to harvesting employee ideas. Each of these Innovation Days is focused on a particular business or function. In advance of the event, a sponsoring vice president personally invites hundreds of employees to submit ideas around a chosen theme—developing novel customer solutions, for instance, or dramatically improving cost efficiency. Accompanying the invitation is a small suite of innovation tools that the participants can use to help stretch their thinking.

A recent Innovation Day focused on ready-mix cement generated more than 250 ideas, which were classified into four categories: *stars* (big ideas that were clearly valuable and could be implemented immediately); *balls* (valuable ideas that needed to be bounced around for a while to see if they were practical); *apples* (good ideas for incremental improvement that could be quickly put into practice); and *bones* (ideas that appeared interesting but, on closer inspection, had little real meat to them). Ten stars emerged from the 250 submissions, including a new way to cast cement that allows contractors to double the returns they get on their investments in the casting molds.

High-profile events that are inclusive can help prime the innovation pump, but to get a steady flow of rule-

changing ideas, organizations will need to institutional-
ize innovation as a deep value. At W.L. Gore, a $1.35 bil-
lion Newark, Delaware–based company with 6,000
employees, the organizational structure, resource allocation practices, and management principles all serve a
single core belief: Innovation can come from anyone,
anywhere. It's hardly surprising that the company places
a premium on serendipity—its signature product, Gore-
Tex, sprang from a humble experiment. Hoping to create
a low-cost plumbers' tape, Bob Gore, the founder's son
and the company's current chairman, stretched a piece
of polytetrafluoroethylene (PTFE) and discovered, quite
by accident, that it had some rather amazing properties.
When PTFE was laminated to fabric, the resulting material was waterproof and breathable—a boon to campers,
hunters, athletes, and many others.

Today, W.L. Gore has no directors, no managers, no
titles, and virtually no hierarchy. (The company refers to
its organizational structure as a lattice.) Employees—
"associates"—don't have bosses; they have sponsors.
Every associate can allocate 10% of his or her time to
dreaming up new applications for the company's unique
materials. When an idea emerges, it's up to the innovator
to recruit colleagues to support its development. This
market for ideas acts as a screening device. Ideas strong
enough to attract volunteers from across the company
move forward; projects with less drawing power don't.
Beyond this, a cross-functional oversight group periodi-
cally meets with project teams to ensure that the ideas
they're pursuing are commercially viable. W.L. Gore's
innovation democracy has propelled the company into
areas as diverse as fuel cells, medical devices, sealants,
dental floss, and guitar strings. It has also made the company one of America's most highly rated employers—not

least because people get to work on projects they care about. The excitement, ardor, and intensity produced by this fusion of vocation and avocation are powerful resource multipliers. W.L. Gore, like Cemex, gets a lot out of its people because it believes there is a lot in them.

What else can you do in addition to asking for and expecting innovation? To begin with, set a goal. Identify the number of people in your company who have an innovation role (R&D personnel, product development staff, and so on). If this group comprises less than 10% of your employee base, commit to tripling that number over the next 12 months—not by hiring more innovation specialists but by involving existing employees in innovation processes or events. Ensure that employees are given the time, tools, and space they'll need to exercise their innovation muscles. Create an Innovation Board that will screen new ideas and sponsor first-stage experiments. For every department and business unit, benchmark the percentage of employees who have submitted ideas or participated in innovation events. Do all this, and your innovation yields will soar.

Look Outside

Regardless of how creative your employees may be, there's more innovation potential outside your company than within it. Look around, and you'll see a world filled with software hackers, music remixers, video producers, and bloggers. Technology is rapidly emancipating the human imagination. The challenge is to harness this imagination in ways that multiply one's own innovation resources. Companies have long sought to complement their internal development efforts with external sources of innovation. Typical strategies have included licensing technology from more innovative firms, polling lead users for new ideas, outsourcing R&D to universities, or joining research consortia. All this is old hat. What's new is the ability to use the Web to tap the world's ever-expanding reservoir of human creativity. Before the Internet, it was hard to find people whose passions matched your problems. No more. Even better, many of these zealous souls are willing to work for a mere pittance.

Consider the development of Linux, the "other" operating system. In 2001, the last time someone counted, Linux had more than 30 million lines of source code, representing something like 8,000 person-years of development time. Had this software been developed by well-compensated software engineers, the bill would have come to roughly $1 billion. Instead, it was created by volunteers—a development model even more efficient than outsourcing work to India's eager young coders. Even IBM, with its multibillion-dollar research budget, finds this deal too good to pass up: Linux is now at the heart of the company's enterprise-computing strategy.

Is Linux a single, shining exception to the do-it-yourself norm? Nope. Epic Games and Digital Extremes, creators of the popular Unreal Tournament computer game, have enrolled thousands of their customers in a virtual development network. Along with NVIDIA, a maker of ultra-fast graphic chip sets, and a handful of other companies, the game companies have sponsored a $1 million competition that rewards individuals from around the world who build eye-popping "mods" and "cons." New mods—in the form of new weapons, characters, and action settings—can be downloaded by game players and thus enrich the gaming experience. Conversions are entirely new games that utilize the Unreal Tournament game engine. Both serve to multiply Epic's own development efforts.

To further fuel the flames of innovation, Epic Games has posted more than 100 hours of free, downloadable video training on its Web site—all designed to help users learn how to create custom game content. In addition, the latest DVD version of Unreal Tournament includes a powerful suite of design tools—some of the same tools used by Epic's internal developers.

Putting this in context, imagine that Chevrolet distributed powerful computer-aided design software with every Corvette it shipped, along with a digital rendering of every fender, valve, piston, wheel, and knob of its signature sports car, and then invited car nuts everywhere to submit their mods and cons. Imagine further that the best of these ideas were posted on Chevy's Web site to inspire yet more innovation among the world's horde of aspiring car designers. If Epic Games can create a volunteer developer network, why not Chevy?

To energize a congregation of volunteers, you must first answer some critical questions. Who out there cares about the problems my company cares about? What kind of investment in this protocommunity would be required to build goodwill and trust? What nonmonetary incentives might engender the volunteers' contributions? What mechanisms—Web sites, peer review processes, discussion forums, standards and protocols, and so on—can we use to structure their contributions?

As ever, it's helpful to set a goal. A.G. Lafley, Procter & Gamble's transformation-minded chairman, has challenged his company to source half its innovations from outside the company, up from roughly 20% at present. Lafley wants more success stories like P&G's Swiffer mop, which uses technology purchased from a Japanese competitor. He understands that P&G's next killer product or business model may come from someone who's not even on the payroll.

Get Radical

For most companies the issue is less, "Are we investing enough in innovation?" and more, "Are we investing enough in ideas with the power to make a real difference to our competitive performance?" The fact is, most "new" ideas are nothing of the sort. They're retreads, updates, and add-ons—modest improvements to ideas that were modest to begin with. To be clear, there's nothing wrong with incrementalism. But it's radical ideas that yield the biggest innovation payoffs and drive above-average growth. An idea is radical if it meets one or more of three tests:

- **It changes customer expectations and behaviors.** For example, PayPal's user-friendly service has changed the way people send money to one another.

- **It changes the basis of competitive advantage.** The proliferation of digital cameras, for instance, has altered the basis for competition in the photographic film industry.

- **It changes industry economics.** For example, with its simplified route structure, no-frills service, and flexible work practices, Southwest Airlines has dramatically changed the traditional cost structure for airlines.

Understand, "radical" doesn't necessarily mean "risky." Risky investments are uncertain and expensive. Some radical ideas, like fusion power, are risky, but many are not. A good example is the Starbucks debit card. The idea was radical: Who, after all, would have expected that coffee drinkers would happily pay for their daily dose of caffeine days or weeks in advance? Yet it wasn't a particularly risky idea. The technology (magnetic-stripe debit cards) was well proven, and the idea could be easily tested in a few stores before a big rollout. The risk may have been small, but the payoff has been big. In the first two months after the card's launch in November 2001, Starbucks booked more than $60 million in prepayments. Since then, more than 26 million cards have been sold, and they now account for about 10% of Starbucks's sales.

French physiologist Claude Bernard once remarked, "It is what we think we know already that often prevents us from learning." To generate radical ideas, you have to teach people to look beyond the conventional. A good way to start is to ask a group of employees to deconstruct your company's business model into its constituent elements: supply chain, value proposition, product configuration, pricing, marketing strategy, and so on. The team members should then conduct a point-by-point comparison with the business models of your biggest competitors. Whenever they identify a point of convergence—and they will find dozens—they should ask, "Is there truly no other way to organize this aspect of our business, or have we become the unwitting prisoners of industry convention?" The goal here is to become conscious of the orthodoxies and the dogmas—the standard industry practices, if you will—that silently strangle radical ideas.

Here's a simple example of an industry dogma. Check in to any midprice hotel, and you will probably find a closet filled with theft-proof hangers. Their loop-and-ball design delivers a brusque message from hotel management: "We know you would steal our hangers if you had the chance." Is there a more profitable and customer-friendly way of handling the problem? Sure. Put a sign in the closet that says, "Hangers: $5. Help yourself." Then ask the person who checks the minibar to count the hangers as well. Voilà—the closet becomes a profit center. That idea, by itself, won't change a hotel chain's fortunes—but a large portfolio of similarly unconventional ideas certainly could. To build such a portfolio, employees must be trained to recognize and challenge any industry practice that is justified by nothing more than precedent.

Discontinuities—in technology, demographics, lifestyle, regulation, and geopolitics—are often the launching pad for radical innovation. But just as individuals can be blind to industry dogma, they can also be oblivious to the implications of deep change. For example, one noteworthy demographic trend in recent years has been the steady increase in the number of single-person households in the United States. Until recently, this trend seems to have been mostly ignored by the appliance industry. While microwave ovens are well suited to the needs of someone living alone, many other appliances are not. Dishwashers, for example, are cavernous, capable of washing the plates, pots, and pans associated with a large family meal. What are the choices for someone living alone? Wash the dishes by hand after every meal? Inefficient. Run the dishwasher with a very small load? Uneconomical. Wait several days until the dishwasher is full of plates covered with an impenetrable crust? Gross. At Whirlpool, a cross-company team studied the changing demographics of the American household and came up with a radically new concept: Why not make a small dishwasher as convenient to use as a microwave oven? The result was Briva, an in-sink dishwasher that can wash and dry a small load of dishes in five minutes.

To find the innovation potential in discontinuities, companies need to ask, "What are the deep changes in our world that our competitors have underestimated or ignored?" This requires less a crystal ball than a concerted effort to understand the revolutionary potential in things that are already changing. Dramatic change always creates opportunities for radical innovation—but only if you're paying attention.

Breakthrough innovation typically focuses on solving problems that customers can barely articulate. Unfortunately, traditional market research seldom reveals perennially unmet needs nor does it lay bare long-accepted vexations. What is required instead is an empathetic, first-person understanding of what it feels like to be a customer, coupled with a willingness to search for eye-opening analogies in other industries. Such an approach often yields novel solutions to seemingly insuperable problems.

Take TiVo as an example. It's cool: Push a button, and you can record any show you like and then watch it any time you like. It's radical: Its ad-skipping feature has struck fear into the heart of every soda-selling, pill-plugging executive. But imagine for a moment that we're still back in a pre-TiVo world. How does one go about generating a TiVo-type insight? Not by talking to TV viewers or by interviewing industry executives. Instead, you might want to draw some analogies from the experience of reading a magazine. No one tells you that a magazine is on only at eight o'clock in the evening. No one compels you to read all the advertisements in a magazine. When you need to take a break, you can simply put the magazine down for a few minutes without fear of missing something. In essence, TiVo has made the experience of watching television much like the experience of reading a magazine. We don't know how the TiVo team came up with its big idea. But even with the benefit of hindsight, this simple analogy would have allowed one to posit the inevitability of a TiVo-like device years before it actually hit the market.

Customer problems often remain invisible because we cannot imagine radical new solutions. Yet a disciplined use of analogy—What if a dishwasher were more like a microwave oven? What if watching TV were more like reading a magazine?—often brings long-ignored problems into sharp focus and points the way to radical solutions.

To get more radical ideas in the pipeline, you need to establish a baseline. Start by identifying every initiative that will burn through more than $250,000 in operating or capital expenses over the coming year. (You can adjust this figure depending on the size of your business.) Rate the initiatives on a scale of one to five, where one denotes a project that does nothing more than perpetuate the status quo and five denotes a project that could surprise both competitors and customers. Unsure of what constitutes a five? Identify the three or four most significant game-changing innovations in your industry over the last few years and use them as a benchmark. At the outset, it is unlikely that more than 10% of the projects in your company's innovation pipeline will deserve a score of four or five. Regardless of the percentage, strive to double it within the next year.

To reach that goal, you're going to have to give your employees the skills to innovate. At Whirlpool, for instance, all 15,000 salaried employees are required to complete a two-hour online course on the basics of business innovation. They are also encouraged to call upon the more than 500 innovation mentors across the company who have received extensive training in how to develop, test, and validate new ideas. It's not enough to just expect your employees to innovate; you must equip them to innovate.

Experiment

As any successful entrepreneur will tell you, radical ideas don't start out as surefire bets. A great idea becomes a commercial success through a recursive process of experimentation and learning. At the start, it's not always easy to tell whether a new idea is "smart stupid" (like trying to get millions of consumers to prepay for their coffee) or "stupid stupid" (like trying to get millions of consumers to buy their coffee online). That's why low-cost, under-the-radar experimentation is so important. It allows a company to fully explore the potential of a radical new idea while avoiding the kind of expensive risk-taking that so often gives innovation a bad name.

A few years back, a team at Shell Chemicals identified an opportunity to radically change the economics of the detergent and fabric softener business. Its idea was simple: Formulate products at the point of sale (in supermarkets) and sell them in reusable containers. In theory, everyone would win: Consumers would get custom formulations in smaller, easier-to-store bottles. Retailers would not have to devote so much shelf space to detergents and softeners of multiple scents and sizes. Reusable packaging would be good for the environment. And

Shell would capture more of the value from the active ingredients it supplies to detergent makers.

The idea seemed compelling from every angle. Shell Chemicals had the resources for a big rollout, but the project team knew there was much to learn. As a start, the team talked a major UK retailer into allowing it to conduct a single in-store experiment. Team members built a prototype dispensing machine that was, to put it crudely, not much more than a tin box containing a 55-gallon drum and a pump. This quick, cheap experiment was enough, however, to validate several hypotheses. Consumers liked the machine. They made repeat purchases and reused their bottles. Store managers liked the idea, too. It saved them valuable space, increased their sales, and, because the Shell team had chosen a simple design, didn't require them to station an employee with a mop near the dispenser.

Over the next few months, the team conducted a second small-scale experiment, this time in China. It remained true to its "learn on the cheap" mantra by turning down a request from a U.S. retailer to "test" by installing machines in 100 stores. Along the way, Shell uncovered challenges. In Europe and Asia, the environmental and space-saving benefits appealed to consumers—but many retail outlets in those countries are too small to justify their investment in the machines. U.S. consumers seem to care much less about recycling and storage issues. And in all geographies, there are unresolved issues around branding.

Whether or not the idea of in-store formulation ever pans out, Shell's commitment to low-cost strategic experimentation has clearly paid off. Despite the passion that swirled around the initial idea, an early large-scale launch would have been a disaster. On the other hand, months of in-house research and financial modeling would have produced few real insights. Quick-and-dirty experimentation allowed Shell to rapidly adjust its business model at very low cost.

As your company works to master the art of low-cost experimentation, it's important to keep several principles in mind. First, understand that strategic experimentation of the kind we have been describing is quite different from traditional product testing. If product testing is akin to putting an individual through a battery of tests to see if he is qualified for a specific job, experimentation is more like giving a junior staffer a series of development opportunities to prepare him for a job he might never have dreamed of. Hence, the scope, philosophies, and methodologies for product testing and strategic experimentation are markedly different. (For a comparison, see the exhibit "When Is a Test Not an Experiment?")

Second, don't try to test everything at once. Identify the most critical hypotheses to be tested—for example, market access and acceptance, technical feasibility, pricing and cost economics. Then rank each hypothesis on two criteria: its importance to the eventual success of the product, service, or business model innovation and the degree of uncertainty it entails. Design the first few experiments to generate learning around those hypotheses that are both critical to success and much in doubt. It's all right to be impatient, but be impatient to learn. Remember, new plays open in Des Moines or San Jose or Indianapolis first, *then* they move to Broadway.

Third, if ultimate success depends on leveraging assets or competencies that reside in the core business, don't delegate the responsibility for experimentation and learning to some kind of corporate new-venture unit or incubator, most of which are little more than orphanages

When Is a Test Not an Experiment?

The terms are often used interchangeably, but traditional product testing and strategic experimentation aren't the same thing. They serve different goals, are based on different philosophies, and employ different methodologies.

	Product Testing	**Experimentation**
Scope	*Product or Service* Product testing focuses on enhancements or extensions to well-established products or services within the context of a mostly static business model.	*Business Model* Strategic experiments seek to explore the merits of a number of inter-related changes to a company's business model.
Philosophy	*Prune* Product testing is typically designed to winnow out potential duds. The basic principle is, "Don't invest in losers."	*Learn* Strategic experiments are designed to create opportunities for iterative learning. The basic principle is, "Don't kill a great idea prematurely."
Methodology	*In Vitro* Product testing takes place in laboratory-like conditions, where new products are subjected to ever more rigorous tests with customer panels. Customers use the products but have no chance to buy them until a formal launch decision has been made.	*In Vivo* Wherever possible, experiments are conducted in live commercial settings where customers can buy the product or service or some reasonable facsimile. The goal is to learn how customers interact with all the elements of the redesigned business model.

for unloved ideas. Instead, make it clear to operating managers that it's their responsibility to parent new strategic experiments. Then set up a corporate-level review mechanism to track the progress of experiments across the firm. At Cemex, for example, a top-level Innovation Committee meets monthly to review the company's portfolio of newborn projects, many of which are housed inside operating units. In our experience, such oversight helps to ensure that fledgling experiments don't get terminated under the pressure of short-term operational goals.

Stick with It

Big shifts in innovation priorities, and start-again, stop-again investment programs, undermine innovation productivity. When it comes to innovation, consistency counts. Over time, small ideas compound, learning from experimentation accumulates, and competencies grow stronger. Teams develop a collective memory and avoid making the same mistakes twice. With this in mind, a company should commit itself to a relatively small number of medium-term innovation goals. Just as important, it should measure its commitment to those goals not in terms of how much it invests but in terms of how persistently it pursues success.

Consider, for example, the race to produce energy-efficient cars—a race that Toyota appears to be winning despite a big, expensive start by General Motors. In the early 1990s, GM bet big on electric vehicles. Eschewing the hybrid approach in which an electric motor complements the work of a gas engine, GM chose to build the EV1, an egg-shaped, all-electric, zero-emissions vehicle. Launched with great fanfare in 1996, the car proved to be a commercial bust. After spending $1 billion on the project and producing only 700 vehicles, the CEO pulled the plug by 1999.

Toyota was more consistent in its pursuit of energy efficiency—and generated less hype—than most of its rivals. After a multiyear development program, the company introduced a hybrid vehicle in Japan in 1997. In 2003, Toyota sold more than 50,000 hybrid vehicles and planned to sell 300,000 annually in the second half of the decade. Meanwhile, GM's first hybrid car was not scheduled to reach the market until 2007. In a testament to Toyota's patient approach to developing ecofriendly cars, Ford announced late in 2003 that it would license hybrid technology from its Japanese competitor—a somewhat surprising move considering that Ford's annual R&D budget was, at the time, nearly 80% bigger than Toyota's.

Being consistent doesn't mean investing in a new idea for a decade or more with no expectation of revenues or profits along the way. Rather, it's about finding a stepwise migration path with clear checkpoints that allow your company to consolidate its progress and recalibrate its direction. Having learned from the ignominious demise of the EV1, GM has adopted a more graduated approach to its investments in fuel-cell–powered vehicles. The company is increasing its investments in stages, as it learns, and it will first test its fuel cell technology in nonautomotive applications where the performance demands and initial financial risks are less daunting. Revolutionary goals and evolutionary steps—that's the recipe for innovation efficiency.

Finally, to be consistent, your company needs to have something to be consistent about. It needs innovation goals that are big enough to be compelling, yet practical enough to be credible; goals that are broad enough to invite contributions from across the firm and beyond, yet specific enough to provide focus. Such goals have the power to multiply individual efforts.

Competitive evolution has always favored companies that can do more with less, and this is as true for innovation as it is for any other function or activity. To produce more growth per dollar of investment, your company must produce more innovation per dollar of investment. This will require a dramatic and permanent improvement in innovation productivity. It's not enough to skimp, scrimp, and save. To become a growth champion, your company must augment, compound, and multiply. It must parlay meager resources into radical, growth-generating innovation. It must learn to innovate boldly and consistently—on the cheap.

Originally published in July–August 2004
Reprint R0407E

Darwin and the Demon

Innovating Within Established Enterprises

GEOFFREY A. MOORE

Executive Summary

AS COMMERCIAL PROCESSES COMMODITIZE in a developed economy, they are outsourced or transferred offshore, leaving onshore companies with unrelenting, Darwinian pressure to come up with the next wave of innovation. But innovation is a broad term. There are many types, from the bally-hooed *disruptive* innovation to more mundane forms such as *process* and *experiential*, which might involve, respectively, doing such things as streamlining the supply chain and delighting customers with small modifications of products. Many executives find it hard to decide which kind to focus on.

The best way to choose is to consider the phases of a market's life span. In a market's earliest phase, a new technology attracts enthusiasts and visionaries. Eventually, the market reaches the Main Street section of its life, when growth slows, flattens, and finally subsides.

Different types of innovation produce more bang for the buck at different points in the life cycle. Disruptive innovation, for example, is rewarded most during the earliest phase. Once the life cycle advances to Main Street, however, the marketplace is no longer willing to yield the revenue or margin gains necessary to fund that type of innovation, so other forms, including process and experiential, yield better returns.

But attempts to change the company's direction are often thwarted by the inertia that success creates. To overcome the inertia demon, managers must introduce new types of innovation while aggressively extracting resources from legacy processes and organizations. By running the two efforts in parallel, they can defeat the demon and renew the company.

A s COMMERCIAL PROCESSES COMMODITIZE in a developed economy, they are outsourced or transferred offshore or both, leaving onshore companies with unrelenting pressure to come up with the next wave of innovation. Failure to innovate equals failure to differentiate equals failure to garner the profits and revenues needed to attract capital investment. It behooves us all to use our brains to get out in front of this Darwinian process.

For starters, we need to appreciate how broad the domain of innovation really is. Sure, it includes the type everyone knows about: disruptive innovation, the stuff of technology legend and Silicon Valley lore. But we should not be blind to the existence of more mundane forms that are equally effective, as the following taxonomy illustrates:

Disruptive Innovation. Gets a great deal of attention, particularly in the press, because markets appear as if from nowhere, creating massive new sources of wealth. It tends to have its roots in technological discontinuities, such as the one that enabled Motorola's rise to prominence with the first generation of cell phones, or in fast-spreading fads like the collector card game Pokémon.

Application Innovation. Takes existing technologies into new markets to serve new purposes, as when Tandem applied its fault-tolerant computers to the banking market to create ATMs and when OnStar took Global Positioning Systems into the automobile market for roadside assistance.

Product Innovation. Takes established offers in established markets to the next level, as when Intel releases a new processor or Toyota a new car. The focus can be on performance increase (Titleist Pro V1 golf balls), cost reduction (HP inkjet printers), usability improvement (Palm handhelds), or any other product enhancement.

Process Innovation. Makes processes for established offers in established markets more effective or efficient. Examples include Dell's streamlining of its PC supply chain and order fulfillment systems, Charles Schwab's migration to online trading, and Wal-Mart's refinement of vendor-managed inventory processes.

Experiential Innovation. Makes surface modifications that improve customers' experience of established products or processes. These can take the form of delighters ("You've got mail!"), satisfiers (superior line management at Disneyland), or reassurers (package tracking from FedEx).

Marketing Innovation. Improves customer-touching processes, be they marketing communications (use of the Web and trailers for viral marketing of *The Lord of the Rings* movie trilogy) or consumer transactions (Amazon's e-commerce mechanisms and eBay's online auctions).

Business Model Innovation. Reframes an established value proposition to the customer or a company's established role in the value chain or both. Examples include chestnuts like Gillette's move from razors to razor blades, IBM's shift to on-demand computing, and Apple's expansion into consumer retailing.

Structural Innovation. Capitalizes on disruption to restructure industry relationships. Innovators like Fidelity and Citigroup, for example, have used the deregulation of financial services to offer broader arrays of products and services to consumers under one umbrella. Nearly overnight, those companies became sophisticated competitors to old-guard banks and insurance companies.

The breadth of this list can be problematic. How are managers and executives to decide where to focus? Which types of innovation should they pursue? There was a time when the notion of core competences was invoked to solve this problem: Pick the things you are best at and focus your resources accordingly. But companies have discovered that being the best at something doesn't guarantee a competitive advantage. A distinctive competence is valuable only if it drives purchase preferences. Customers frequently ignore companies' core competences in favor of products that are good enough and cheaper.

Riding the Life Cycle

A more reliable way to solve the problem of focus is to think of different types of innovation as being privileged at different points in a market's life. The technology sector has provided ample material for studying the early phases of market development, and I've previously described how those phases can be viewed through the lens of the *technology adoption life cycle* (see the left side of the graphic in the exhibit "The Market Development Life Cycle"). By combining graphical representations of that cycle and of what happens later when markets become more established, we can show market development end to end. The market development life cycle includes the following phases (the first four constitute the technology adoption life cycle for emerging markets):

Early Market. When a technology is introduced, it attracts the attention of early adopters—enthusiasts (who see it as cool) and visionaries (who see it as potentially disruptive). Pragmatic buyers are curious but make no commitments. The press, fascinated, writes glowing articles describing the technology as the next big thing.

The Chasm. The technology is caught betwixt and between. Because it has been in the marketplace for some time and has lost its novelty, visionaries are no longer making big bets on it. But its acceptance isn't widespread enough to convince pragmatists that it would be a safe purchase. Adoption is stalled, and typically the only way for vendors to move forward is to target a niche market that suffers from a nasty problem for which the technology is the sole solution. The "pragmatists in pain" in such a market are the only customers motivated to help the new technology cross the chasm. Current examples of technologies in the chasm include third-generation wireless, on-demand computing, and fuel cells.

Bowling Alley. The technology is gaining acceptance among pragmatists in one or more niche markets where it enables a solution to a nasty problem (when a niche adopts the technology, adjacent niches become more susceptible—hence the bowling pin metaphor). Within

The *Market Development Life Cycle*

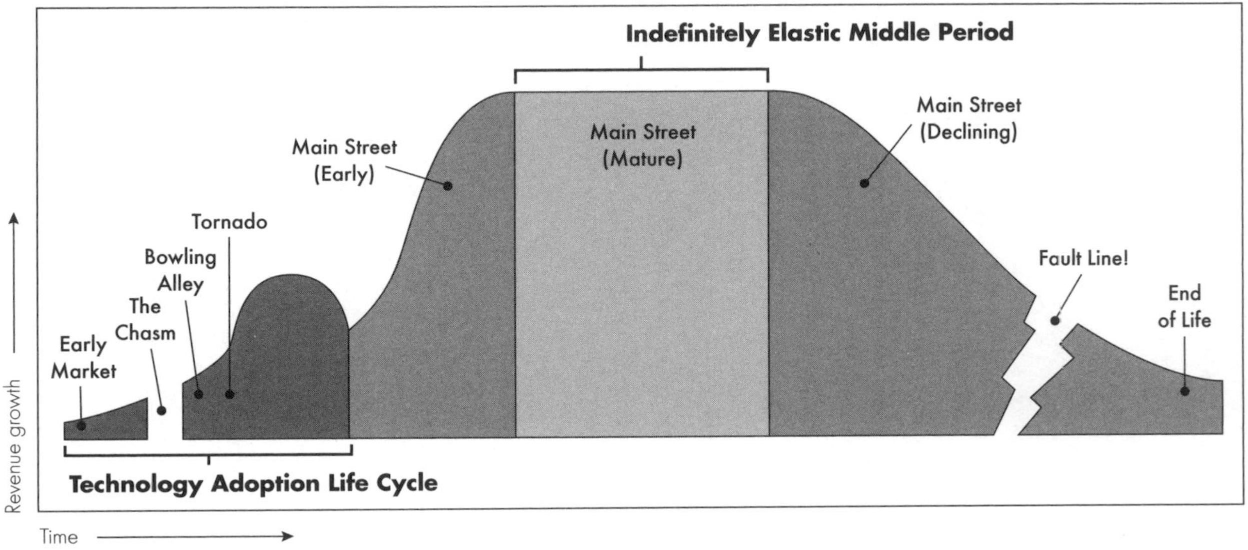

Indefinitely Elastic Middle Period

Main Street (Declining)

Fault Line!

End of Life

Main Street (Mature)

Main Street (Early)

Tornado

Bowling Alley

The Chasm

Early Market

Technology Adoption Life Cycle

Revenue growth

Time

each niche, it is building a loyal following and attracting partners who see a market in the making. Outside the niches, it is still largely unknown.

Tornado. The technology has passed the test of usefulness and is now perceived as necessary and standard for many applications. All the pragmatists who were hanging back from committing are rushing into the market to make sure they don't get left behind. Customers of many types from many fields are making their first purchases of the technology, and revenues are growing at double- or even triple-digit rates. Competition is fierce, with investors bidding up the stock of every company that can participate in the category.

Main Street (Early). The era of hypergrowth has subsided, but the category is still growing nicely. A first wave of consolidation results in a market-share pecking order that is unlikely to change for a long time. Even the companies with small market shares are typically performing well. Customers are focused on seeing systematic improvements in the offering and reward each with an uptick in purchasing.

Main Street (Mature). Category growth has flattened, and commoditization is increasing. A second wave of consolidation thins out the bottom of the pecking order, with market leaders creating top-line growth both organically and through M&A. Customers now take the category for granted, and the press no longer writes about it. On the plus side, however, there are no obsoleting technologies on the horizon, so market risk is at a nadir.

Main Street (Declining). The category has become ossified, and the market dominators are unresponsive to customer needs. Customers are actively looking for relief, a development that is attracting entrepreneurs. The next-generation technologies are on the horizon, although none has gone through the tornado. The market is ripe for some form of disruption, either through an obsoleting technology or a radically innovative business model.

Fault Line and End of Life. Technology obsolescence has struck like an earthquake, exposing the fault line between what the company sells and what the market now desires. The next-generation tornado is wreaking havoc on the installed bases of the established vendors. There is no path forward for companies that produce the obsolete technology, and the only question left is how much money existing customers are willing to spend on the category before it vanishes altogether. Leveraged buyouts become an attractive mechanism for monetizing this remaining market opportunity.

Seeing the Whole Picture

If we overlay our catalog of innovation types onto the market life-cycle model, we can see that at each stage, management has different resources to bring to the challenge of competing for revenues and profit margins. (See the exhibit "Aligning Innovation with the Life Cycle.")

The first three innovation types—disruptive, application, and product—dominate the technology adoption life cycle, interoperating to bring about the creation of the new market category. Until the tornado has blown itself out, no other kind of innovation focus is rewarded.

Once the market moves onto Main Street, however, these forms of innovation lose their leverage. Any delta in competitive advantage they might produce wouldn't be worth the resources required. To put it another way, the marketplace is no longer willing to yield the revenue or margin gains necessary to fund such efforts. (Invest-

Aligning Innovation with the *Life Cycle*

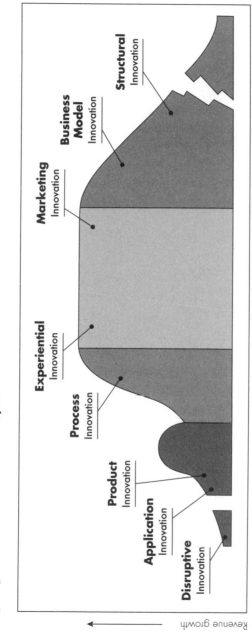

Disruptive Innovation

Application Innovation

Product Innovation

Process Innovation

Experiential Innovation

Marketing Innovation

Business Model Innovation

Structural Innovation

Revenue growth

Time

ments in these types of innovation during the Main Street phases of the market's life have the effect of accelerating commoditization through a process Clay Christensen has called *overshooting*.)

At this point in the market's evolution, a second suite of innovation types comes to the fore—the group consisting of process, experiential, and marketing. Again, the three types can interoperate, and thus they can be used separately or together to create incremental improvements. Sooner or later, even these forms of innovation lose their usefulness and the market moves into an inevitable decline, often with the further threat of an obsoleting technology on the horizon. But companies still have two types of innovation left to exploit: business model and structural.

As markets are commoditizing at one point in the value chain, they are decommoditizing somewhere else (another fine insight from Mr. Christensen). For example, in the automotive industry today, normal maintenance is commoditizing as roadside services are decommoditizing. A nimble enterprise may be able to leverage its reputation with customers to reinvent itself and address their needs in a dramatically different fashion. In its mild form, reinvention grafts a new business model onto the old infrastructure. In its draconian form, it involves a radical restructuring of the enterprise. It's a high-risk endeavor either way, but with the market nearing the fault line, reinvention is the only path forward. The alternative is for executives to call the game over, accept that the market is at the end of its life, and allow the company to be bought by investors who plan to focus on distributing rather than reinvesting the remaining free cash flows.

All in all, then, despite the commoditizing pressures of globalization, management has a surprisingly robust set of opportunities to create shareholder value. Yet few CEOs sleep easy, for their dreams of success are haunted by an unnerving specter, the demon of inertia.

Battling Inertia

The implication of the life-cycle model is that enterprises must mutate their core competences over time to sustain attractive returns. Product-innovation skill, which serves a company wonderfully in a market's early stages, will not sustain it on Main Street, where new expertise in process management and marketing is needed. But management's efforts to change direction are thwarted by the inertia that success creates. The deeper the enterprise is into the life cycle and the more successful it has been, the greater its tendency to return to its former course. For most executive teams, battling the inertia demon is the biggest challenge they face. Sad to say, the demon usually wins.

To overcome inertia, management must introduce new types of innovation while deconstructing old processes and organizations. The most common mistake executive teams make when they seek to introduce change is leaving legacy structures untouched. Their hope is that the success of the new will draw resources away from the old and allow change to occur organically and painlessly. This approach has little chance to succeed. The way to move forward is to aggressively extract resources from legacy processes and organizations and repurpose them to serve the new innovation type, or, if that's not possible, take them out of the company altogether.

So management must pursue a twofold path of concurrent construction and deconstruction. For construction, the goal is to create the next generation of competitive advantage, so the focus should be on the innovation team. It should be sponsored by a senior executive and led by someone who is passionate about, and expert in, the new type of innovation. The choice of sponsor and leader will depend on which type of innovation the team is pursuing, as the exhibit "Choosing the Right Leader" illustrates.

Note how executive sponsorship migrates over the life cycle. During the middle part of a category's life, innovation can be sponsored at the VP level. But it needs the attention of the general manager during the early part of the market's development, and the company-transforming innovations of the late stages demand the full support of the CEO. The team leader should probably be recruited from outside the firm, because he or she must be a world-class performer—and the company's best talent is usually associated with its legacy competences. The rest of the team, by contrast, should be made

Choosing the Right Leader

Innovation Type	Team's Executive Sponsor	Best Team leader
Disruptive	General manager	Entrepreneur (any function)
Application	General manager	Marketing manager
Product	General manager	Engineering manager
Process	VP for operations	Operations manager
Experiential	VP for marketing	Customer service manager
Marketing	VP for marketing	Marketing manager
Business model	CEO	General manager
Structural	CEO	General manager

up of high-potential individuals from inside so that the new effort is grounded in the realities of the business and, over the long term, human capital is extracted from the legacy processes.

Defeating the Demon

The challenge of deconstruction is that the legacy work still needs to be done, but because it no longer drives customer purchase preferences, resources deployed in support of it do not improve market results. These resources are merely preventing the downside consequences of underperformance. Legacy deconstruction should therefore be driven by a simple mantra: Productivity, not differentiation. Differentiation that does not drive customer preference is a liability. Once a company's people fully internalize this principle, the path forward is clear:

1. *Centralize the function.* Legacy processes are typically embedded in each of the enterprise's operating units. Bring them together under a shared-services model, and put an operations-focused manager in charge. This will free resources that are performing duplicate functions.

2. *Standardize the process.* More often than not, processes pulled together into a shared-services model retain their idiosyncrasies. Invoke the mantra to standardize them into a single process set. Users will scream. Plug your ears. The resources that are no longer needed for maintaining multiple versions will more than pay for your troubles.

3. *Simplify the process.* Once processes have been standardized, they can be simplified in a leveraged way.

Just make sure that during the course of process redesign, people do not try to innovate (it is a powerful human urge, after all). The idea is to take resources out, not put more in.

4. *Automate or outsource the process.* Make the processes go away, either by embedding them in computer transactions or exporting them to a firm for which they will be a source of revenue instead of a drag on profits. Because you have already centralized, standardized, and simplified, the good news here is that you have reduced both the expense and risk of this step.

It's important to recognize that differentiation-creating innovation and productivity-creating deconstruction must be conducted in tandem. If you try the former without the latter, the inertia demon defeats you. If you try the latter without the former, you do nothing to overcome the forces of commoditization; you are simply able to endure them longer. By running the two efforts in parallel, and migrating resources from legacy processes to innovation wherever possible, you not only improve your returns in the marketplace, you renew and rejuvenate the company. Neither Darwin's forces nor the demon's will defeat you.

Originally published in July–August 2004
Reprint R0407F

Selling to the Moneyed Masses

PAUL F. NUNES, BRIAN A. JOHNSON,
AND R. TIMOTHY S. BREENE

Executive Summary

OVER THE PAST DECADE, the distribution of household incomes has shifted so much that a much larger proportion of consumers now earn significantly higher-than-average incomes—while still falling short of being truly rich. As a result, what used to be a no-man's-land for new product introductions has in many categories become an extremely profitable "new middle ground."

How can marketers capitalize on this new territory? The key, say the authors, is to rethink the positioning and design of offerings and the ways they can be brought to market.

Take, for instance, how Procter & Gamble redefined the positioning map for tooth-whitening solutions. A decade ago, dental centers were popularizing expensive bleaching techniques that put the price of a professionally brightened smile in the $400 range. At the low end, consumers also had the choice of whitening tooth-pastes that cost anywhere from $2 to $8. P&G wisely positioned itself between the two ends, successfully targeting the new mass market with its $35 Whitestrips.

In product categories where it's clear the middle ground has already been populated, it's important for companies to design or redesign offerings to compete. An example is the Polo shirt. How do you sell a man yet another one after he's bought every color he wants? Add some features, and call it a golf shirt. Here, marketers have introduced designs based on the concept of "occasional use" in order to stand out.

Finally, companies wishing to reach the "almost rich" can change how they go to market. Perhaps no mass retailer has made a stronger bid for the mass affluent than Target Stores, which has pioneered a focus the company itself characterizes as upscale discount. The strategy has made Target an everyday shopping phenomenon among well-heeled urbanites and prosperous professionals.

Q UICK QUESTION: What do Whitestrips, the Spin-Brush, and the Swiffer have in common? Aside from the fact they're all made by Procter & Gamble, all have launched new billion-dollar industries in categories that have been stagnant—some would say dead—for many years. In addition, they all have price points that are multiples higher than their competitors on the shelves—and simultaneously many times lower than the high-end solutions to the problems they address. And they all share enviable margins—three to five times higher than the market leaders they supersede.

Yet one of the most interesting things all three products have in common is what's *absent*: any evidence of microtargeting. These offerings didn't come about because a company zeroed in on profitable customer subsegments. Quite the contrary: They are generic, expected to serve millions of consumers across multiple traditional segments. In other words, in a commercial environment smitten with CRM and "markets of one," they are unabashedly mass market.

In this article, we argue that products like Whitestrips, the SpinBrush, and the Swiffer are only the beginning. Thanks to a dramatic shift in the distribution of U.S. household incomes, a whole new tier of mass market offerings suddenly makes sense. A vast new middle ground has opened up between what previously constituted the mass and high-end choices, and for many companies, capturing that ground is the most promising route to profitable growth. This is exactly what P&G has set out to do, and that's why it's no fluke that our first three examples come from that company. In a 2003 earnings conference call, Procter & Gamble CEO A.G. Lafley put it this way: "One of the things we focus on when we try to grow a new category or create a new category, and this is what we did with whitening, is we try to bring things out of the professional area, and I'm not talking about brands, but I'm talking about habits and practices that you can do at home with less risk, more ease, and all the rest of it." He went on to mention hair coloring, where P&G was innovating at the moment, but the point was that the same kind of middle-ground strategy could be pursued in many, many other markets.

Similar opportunity exists in your business, too. But to capitalize on it, first you'll need to rethink how to position your offerings and even reconsider the entire "position map" of your industry. Next, you'll have to design or modify your offerings with a more affluent mass market in mind. And finally, you'll need to adjust how you go to market, in terms of both retail channels and promotions. In the sections that follow, we'll explore these three challenges and how some companies are addressing them with imagination and style. Their experiences make one thing clear: Success at mass marketing comes not from obeying its timeworn rules but from reinventing the rules for today's mass market.

The New Shape of the Mass Market

A funny thing happened to U.S. household income while marketers weren't looking: Its distribution curve changed dramatically. (See the graph in the exhibit "The Emergence of Mass Affluence.") It used to be that incomes clustered intensely at or near the average level. A huge proportion of households, in other words, made essentially the same amount of money. Past that hump, the numbers of households earning at greater increments dropped off precipitously. But note the change since 1970. That cliff no longer exists; in its place is an attenuated slope. What this means for marketers is that a vast new space has opened up for offerings that were once not economical enough to pursue.

Under the old income distribution, there were two kinds of offerings: affordably priced mainstream offerings for the middle wage earner (think $2 toothpastes and toothbrushes) and luxury or professional offerings priced so high that only a very small number of buyers indulged in them (think $1,000 tooth-whitening treatments). For companies operating in any given category of goods or services, having offerings in these two distinct markets meant the marketplace was fully served. Now, however, there are enough people earning at increments between the average and the top incomes that many market positions in between are economically viable. (SpinBrush: $10. Whitestrips: $35.) Therefore, the company that still considers the markets of the very rich and the masses to be two distinct markets is undoubtedly leaving a lot of money on the table.

A look at the exhibit "Consumer Spending by Top Earners" gives a sense of just how much money is on the table. It shows that, despite the income increases many U.S. households have experienced during the last 30 years, their spending has not kept pace. The top quintile (households earning over $68,522 in 1984 and $84,016 in 2002, in 2002 real dollars) used to spend roughly 74% of their income. They now spend just 66% of it. As a result, the top-earning households now account for 49% of the total income in the United States, but only 37% of total spending. To be sure, the increased marginal utility of saving in a rising market explains some of that difference, as does the fact that higher-income earners are always in a better position to save. Possibly, some families who have been very well-off are suffering economic anxieties today and are being cautious about their spending. Still, the fact that consumption expenditures have lagged so dramatically behind earnings growth suggests a failure by marketers to address, or better stimulate, these households' needs and desires.

And where *have* marketers been looking, to have missed these broad market trends? They've been relentlessly focused on increasingly narrow segments of their customer base. For decades, marketing theory and practice have been moving toward the "market of one";

The Emergence of Mass Affluence

Between 1970 and 2000, a major shift took place in the distribution of U.S. household earnings. Few experts have noted that shift in part because they're used to seeing distorted income distribution curves. For whatever reason, the U.S. Census information we often see graphed uses an x-axis with unequal increments. The amount of horizontal space used to represent a $5,000 difference in income is collapsed and expanded in such a way that the distribution takes on the appearance of a bell curve. People who see such versions can be forgiven for believing that income in the U.S. is fairly normally distributed. Our version holds the increments on the x-axis constant, revealing what economists know to be the truth about U.S. income distribution: that it is a log-normal distribution, high on the left, followed by a steep slope down.

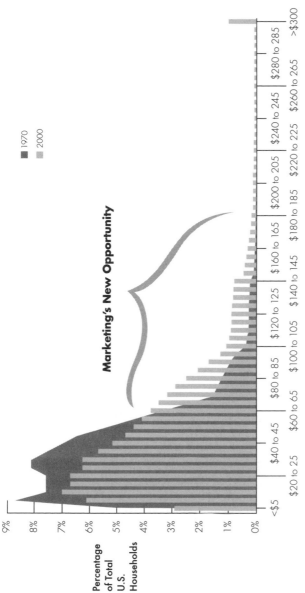

Marketing's New Opportunity

Percentage of Total U.S. Households

1970
2000

Household Income (in thousands)

<$5 $20 to 25 $40 to 45 $60 to 65 $80 to 85 $100 to 105 $120 to 125 $140 145 $160 to 165 $180 185 $200 to 205 $220 to 225 $240 to 245 $260 to 265 $280 to 285   >$300

0%   1%   2%   3%   4%   5%   6%   7%   8%   9%

Note: All values in 2000 CPI-U-RS dollars (real dollars). Incremental values interpolated from larger increments when not available.

Source: U.S. Census Bureau, Money Income in the United States: 2000, September 2001.

Consumer Spending by Top Earners

This bar chart shows average household expenditure as a percentage of income (before taxes) * for the top 20% of earners in the United States. Despite the rollercoaster pattern from 1984 to 2002, spending overall has followed a downward trajectory.

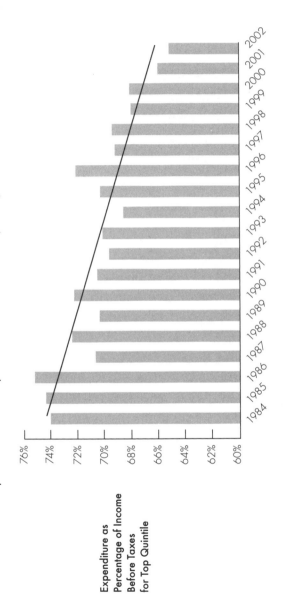

Expenditure as
Percentage of Income
Before Taxes
for Top Quintile

*Results are nearly identical when using after-tax numbers.

Source: U.S. Bureau of Labor Statistics, Consumer Expenditure Survey 1984 to 2002.

modern companies have learned to think in terms of "customer-centricity." Marketers have the tools now to separate out great customers from good customers from merely okay customers—and to focus their attention on the most valuable tiers. But in the single-minded pursuit of wallet share, they've failed to see the forest for the triage.

Even the few who have perceived the shift may have missed its import. What we are seeing is a ratcheting up of income levels—a new "mass affluence," as it's been called. At first glance, we might simply think that goods are being consumed in greater quantity or that prices of basic products are now rising in step with income. But what's happening is more fundamental than that. At a certain point, a saturation level is reached. Once our houses are warm, we don't make them uncomfortably hot just because we have the money. With such affluence, U.S. consumers don't buy more of what they already have, and they're certainly no longer concentrating on subsistence and fighting the elements. There has been a step change, and we are now operating at a higher level in Maslow's famous hierarchy of needs. If John Kenneth Galbraith was right in calling us an affluent society in 1958, then surely by now we are a mature or even postaffluent society. Whatever the terminology, we have entered a new era marked by a new psychology of selling and consumption. As with any societal shift, there are people in the vanguard, but we're at the point now that the shift is becoming a mass phenomenon.

Repositioning and the New Middle Ground

What does the new shape of today's market mean to consumer goods companies? For most of them, the best

chances for growth lie not in increased microsegmenta-
tion but in an updated form of mass marketing—with its
central tenets continuing to be scale production and
sales largely to anonymous customers. Note that we are
not recommending that managers simply return to traditional mass-marketing approaches. Rather, they should
practice a new approach: one that looks to the basic
components of mass marketing—positioning, the design
of offerings, and go-to-market strategies—but that refor-
mulates them with the new, moneyed masses in mind.
(See the table "Seven Ways to Tap the Mass Affluent.")

Let's start with positioning, where most marketers
will recognize the conventional wisdom by its initials:
STP. The order of business has been to *segment* customers first, then *target* the attractive segments, and
then *position* offerings accordingly. It remains a reasonable approach, but the problem is, it can quickly lead to
very small segments. And while those valuable customers will buy more enhanced offerings, the various
enhancements will not add up to something with broad
appeal. Rather than go down those rabbit holes, we're
recommending that marketers try to make a positioning
decision before they target and segment. We base that
recommendation on a broad survey we conducted in
2002 of more than 3,500 consumers, who told us that
when they shopped, they often found that they had to
choose between products that cost less than they were
willing to pay and were not satisfying their needs and
products that were too expensive. They perceived a large
gap, in other words, between the run-of-the-mill mass
market offerings and the high-end luxury offerings.

Of course, that gap was always there, but consumers
now feel it more. And ironically, the fact that consumers
are chafing about it reflects that it is a smaller gap than it

Seven Ways to Tap the Mass Affluent

Components of Mass Marketing	The Old Rules		Seven New Rules	Examples
Positioning Offerings	Avoid middle-market positions between low-cost and premium.	1	Seize the new middle-ground position: above the best of the conventional offerings and below ultrapremium solutions.	"No wrinkle" shirts, like those from Brooks Brothers and Lands' End, fill the gap between polyester blends and laundered 100% cotton shirts.
	Provide identical offerings at a price affordable to all.	2	Provide nearly identical offerings to all, at prices they can afford.	For an annual fee of $50, Hertz grants even infrequent renters "#1 Club Gold" status. With their preferences on record, club members bypass the line at the airport counter.
Designing Offerings	Make the "special" suitable for everyday use by the masses.	3	Make versions of "everyday" products that are suitable only for special-use occasions.	Starbucks's "After Coffee" mints and gum command prices two to ten times those of their multiuse brethren, and their sales exceed competitors', too.
	Produce less-expensive versions of luxuries to sell to the masses.	4	Introduce new models of ownership that make real luxuries affordable to the masses.	Fractional ownership has made luxuries like high-end cars, homes, and art available to millions of consumers.
	Offer the masses new consumables and new investment opportunities.	5	Offer new consumables that perform like investments.	Watchmaker Patek Philippe reminds buyers that its watches are not owned, just kept safe for the next generation.
Reaching Customers	Make retail stores destinations for the masses by having the biggest varieties and discounts	6	Serve the masses locally, with the convenience, layout, and assortment you know they want and the prices you know they will pay.	Retailers like Wal-Mart, Best Buy, and Home Depot are using smaller store formats to get closer to the urban affluent.
	Keep spending on promotion until the masses are convinced they want your offering.	7	Limit the need for spending on promotion by becoming highly relevant to the masses.	NBC modified its lineup and program content to attract a viewing audience who is more affluent and therefore more valuable to advertisers.

used to be. Here's why. Consider tooth-whitening solutions, in which the highest-end functionality two decades ago was a complicated and expensive capping procedure performed by dentists. Meanwhile, the category position where most toothpaste makers were competing was around a $2 price point. Innovation by the mass marketers focused on improving whitening performance, and that led to marginally higher price points. Tom's of Maine, with exotic ingredients like propolis and myrrh, now fetches about $5 per tube. Rembrandt is almost $8. But over the same period, dental centers were popularizing new bleaching techniques that put the price of a professionally brightened smile in the $400 range, as opposed to the $1,000 it might have cost before. At that price point, an offering is still not an everyday expense, but for the newly moneyed masses, it does become an option—and suddenly, the consumer is keenly aware of the middle ground between the two ends of the spectrum. Procter & Gamble moved into this middle ground first with its $35 Whitestrips.

The new middle ground is now emerging in other product categories. Many marketers, however, fail to see it because they continue to draw positioning maps in traditional ways. Consider what a Kraft Foods marketer said about the company's decision to launch its DiGiorno line of frozen pizzas. In 1996, frozen pizza was a 50 cent to $2.50 proposition, and the brands at the top of that range were considered high-end. Mary Kay Haben, whose work on DiGiorno made her *Brandweek's* "marketer of the year," told that magazine, "When we first started, there was that initial skepticism. Will anybody pay $5.59 for a frozen pizza given that they're used to getting two for $5?" The key was what had been happening in the restaurant pizza business in the years just prior. Home delivery (the high-end product) had dropped to a $7 price point, making it a weekly habit for many families and not an occasional indulgence. Marketers might not have noticed, but the position map had been reframed, so that what had been a no-man's-land between the professional and mass market offering was now a middle ground to be seized—in this case, frozen pizzas of pizza-parlor quality that cost between $2.50 and $7.

How do you find a new middle ground in your own category? Here's an exercise that might help. First, identify all the benefits your existing offering delivers. Then consider all the really expensive high-end offerings out on the market that satisfy the customer needs that your product does. This expands the positioning map. (In their book *Why Not?*, innovation scholars Barry Nalebuff and Ian Ayres refer to this as imagining, "What would Croesus do?") Next, pick a price point that is substantially higher than your category's average (anywhere from two to ten times higher is a good start) but still below the high-end solution, and then imagine what you could possibly offer given the freedom to spend—on development as well as delivery—what these price points would give you. What unmet customer needs could be addressed, and what innovative approaches might be considered, if you were expecting to make that kind of money? This should lead to ideas like creating a $10 battery-operated toothbrush—positioned well below $60 rechargeable ones but well above the $3 or so upper limit for manual toothbrushes—as opposed to finding yet another way to angle bristles on a $2 brush.

In certain cases, delivering the extra value will mean giving consumers enhanced access to your offering. This is what Copper Mountain, a ski resort in Colorado, has done with its Beeline Advantage program. Those willing to pay $124 for a day of skiing, roughly twice the normal lift ticket price, enjoy two advantages: They get the first runs of the morning on fresh powder (because the mountain is open 15 minutes early for them), and they spend less time in lift lines (thanks to specially designated Beeline queues). This kind of repositioning makes sense to companies that have tremendous sunk costs in their existing assets and lack the flexibility to come up with fundamentally new products. Universal Studios Theme Parks had the same insight that, because a day could not be made longer, the way to enhance the offering would be to let people spend less of that day standing in line. The standard one-day pass at its Hollywood park is $49, but for $99 you can purchase a "Front of Line Pass," and for $129, a "VIP Experience," including special behind-the-scenes access to facilities.

It's not an idea that's limited to recreation destinations. Dell has been testing a Priority Call Routing program that allows customers to pay $89 and for three years have their calls for technical support moved to the front of the line.

Other companies are successfully selling status—that is, the privileged tier of service that once came only with loyal patronage. Rental car agencies were among the earliest companies to sell this better treatment outright, regardless of usage level, for an annual fee. Now companies from airlines to restaurants are following suit. It makes sense. Some customers who don't do a large volume of business with a company still value the extras enough to pay for them. In fact, customers with low usage levels who pay for recognition are potentially more profitable than loyal customers, who are likely to take fuller, more-frequent advantage of a company's perks.

Selling access in these ways is not without risks. Marketing academics have noted that the opportunity for such "discriminatory pricing" works best with goods and services that are frivolous in nature. Applying such pricing to items regarded as necessities is likely to spur a negative reaction from consumers. Indeed, our research confirmed that most consumers are somewhat uncomfortable with companies creating differentiated offerings in most categories. This may be changing, however. Hospitals routinely permit patients to pay extra for private rooms; some maternity wards offer suites to rival the Four Seasons. And a private company called MDVIP has been growing steadily since its launch in 2000 with a model not unlike Dell's. Patients who pay up front to be members get faster access to and more face time with their physicians.

Redesigning Offerings for the Mass Affluent

Once it's clear there is a new middle ground in a category, a key challenge becomes designing or redesigning an offering to appeal to the mass affluent. Companies will find they can make highly effective changes in any of three core areas: They can alter the consumption context of their product, its payment or exchange model, or its value proposition to the customer.

Changing the consumption context means finding new situations or conditions in which your product can perform and then making subtle alterations to fit those circumstances. A perfect example is Nike's successful marketing of a shoe especially suited to water sports. It's an interesting story because the innovation was somewhat serendipitous. Nike noticed that one of its lightweight running shoes, which had been a failure in

the broader market, had become a favorite of wind-
surfers. The shoe provided traction in the water and
cushion against rough ground, but it didn't get water-
logged enough to weigh down a person's foot. The company made some quick modifications to the shape,
added neon colors, and voilà—the Aqua Sock was born.
The first 50,000 pairs sold out in less than a month, and
production quickly jumped to 3,000 pairs a day.

This type of marketing, which is perfectly suited to
reaching the moneyed masses, is quite different from the
mass marketing of the past. Before, the key was to find
products that could cut across consumption contexts.
Polo shirts were a hit because they fit into many occasions. But how do you sell a man yet another polo shirt
once he's bought every color he wants? Add some features, and call it a golf shirt! This focus on what we call
"occasional use" has been employed by wineglass maker
Riedel. While the Austrian firm has been in the glass
business for nearly 300 years, its growth hit a new trajectory after Claus Riedel introduced a series of ten glasses,
each shaped and sized to do justice to a particular type
of wine. The innovation further narrowed the occasion of
use for what seemed to be an already distinctly tailored
product, the wineglass. That was in 1973. Today, Riedel
offers more than 80 different glasses, ranging from $8 to
$85 per stem, and sells over five million of them annually.

This isn't as frivolous as it may appear. If you know an
avid woodworker, for example, you know how he covets
that 3/8" spindle gouge—or whatever highly specialized
device he lacks. Everyone enjoys using the right tool for
the right job. The key is to understand that, due to mass
affluence, the opportunity to serve that desire is height-
ened. Not only do people have the wherewithal to buy
specially designed risotto pots, they also find themselves

in a broader range of contexts in which such products would make sense. Consider that, in decades past, activities for the rich and poor alike tended to be more circumscribed. The rich had more activities, perhaps, but they still hewed to a certain lifestyle. Today, mass affluence means a man is as likely to need a tuxedo as a bowling shirt. And new versions of everyday products, designed for special-use occasions, are now a major growth opportunity.

A second way to modify your offering in light of today's mass affluence is to rethink the offering's exchange model—that is, how it is paid for—and more broadly, what it means to own the good. What if there were no givens in your category as to rights of ownership, payment options, or expected duration of ownership? A Chicago-based company called Exotic Car Share assumed just that and created a new equity ownership program for rare, antique, and luxury automobiles. The program makes it possible to buy a one-fifth share in a Ferrari 360 Modena Spider, for example, or Lamborghini Murciélago or Bentley Arnage T. For founder George Kiebala, the business model was a natural extension of the fractional ownership already common in jets, vacation properties, and even yachts. As with those goods, his company's offering made a genuine luxury accessible to a whole new tier of buyers.

Beyond reducing price points, this kind of arrangement responds more deeply to the needs of today's moneyed masses. They are discovering what the megarich have often observed (without getting much sympathy): that ownership has its burdens. Every oceanfront home, vintage car, or precious piece of art requires care—so much that it often seems you don't own your possessions, they own you. Marketers would do well to consider

that problem carefully, because the upkeep of possessions is no longer a problem for the megarich alone.
Many of us who cannot afford full-time household managers have amassed unprecedented numbers of material
goods, from computing and entertainment systems to
snowblowers and cappuccino makers—and we have less
time to care for our possessions than we did in the past.
(Americans, on average, worked almost 100 hours more
per year in 2000 than they did in 1980.) What's more,
there's a growing "claustrophobia of abundance," asserts
marketing consultancy Yankelovich Partners, caused by
the fact that "people just feel overwhelmed by [their]
stuff." There's a reason that California Closets, which
customizes storage solutions for home owners, grew six-
fold from 1996 to 2002.

Ownership can be less onerous, too, when it doesn't
endure as long. This is why international retailer IKEA is
working to change consumers' attitudes about furniture
purchases. Its $50 million TV advertising campaign sati-
rizes the sentimental attachments people have to old,
and often ugly, home goods. When the ads' protagonists
replace their furniture, a narrator chastises viewers for
taking pity on the old items. "You are crazy," he tells the
audience. IKEA marketer Christian Mathieu talked
about the impetus for the campaign in a recent conversation. "We considered how Swatch, for example,
changed its category," he said. "The company trans-
formed watches from rare purchases into more affordable items that consumers bought as fashion state-
ments." If furniture and watches can change, why not
rethink the ownership models of other categories? Jewelry and art come to mind as other opportunities. In both
cases, high cost is only one reason a customer might be
disinclined to buy; another is the prospect of having to

live with one's choice. Slowly a market is forming (part of which is a viable resale market) to allow consumers to lease original artworks just as they do automobiles.

A third way to rethink and renovate offerings is in terms of their value proposition to buyers. Marketers must realize that, as people become wealthier, they adopt more of an investment mind-set. They do, of course, invest more in financial instruments than the less affluent. But at the same time, many of the things the truly wealthy buy appreciate in value. The implication for marketers is that it will be easier to sell to the mass affluent market if they can make their products perform more like investments. Note that apparel retailer Talbots, which surely targets the mass affluent buyer, uses the term "dividends" to describe its frequent shopper program, reinforcing the company's commitment to offering valuable, investment-quality clothing.

Allen-Edmonds, a maker of high-end men's shoes, provides a slightly different kind of investment appeal by offering customers a "recrafting" service. For about half what a man would pay for a new pair of Allen-Edmonds shoes, he can have his current pair refurbished and looking as good as ever. At the outset, the idea of offering such a service was controversial within the company; the risk of cannibalizing new sales is an obvious one. In practice, however, the approach has paid off on three fronts. The promise of recrafting (and what it signals about the intrinsic quality of the shoe) increases the value proposition, driving increased initial sales. The need to drop off worn shoes for recrafting at a retail outlet means more traffic in the stores. And, critically, recrafting yields higher margins than original manufacture does. If you thought buyers of expensive shoes wouldn't bother getting them fixed, then you don't know the moneyed masses. Lou Ripple, Allen-Edmonds's director of sales and marketing, told us, "It's not unheard of for us to have customers recraft the same pair of shoes five or six times."

Reaching the Nouveau Niche

So far in this article, we've proposed new rules for positioning and designing offerings to suit today's consumers. What's left to examine is the challenge of going to market. Finding the right retail channels to bring goods to the masses has always been difficult, and like so much of mass marketing, it needs to be rethought for the current era.

The imperative for retailers is clear. They must preserve the proven advantages that have brought them mass market success so far—customer-facing features like accessibility, selection, and service, and operational features like supply-chain efficiency—while also serving a far more diverse and upscale set of needs. That means making a direct appeal to more affluent consumers, with steps ranging from determining and delivering better in-store assortments, to creating more highly tailored, conveniently located retail outlets.

At the most basic level, we see stores expanding the upper end of their assortments. Perhaps no mass retailer has made a stronger bid for mass affluent consumers than Target Stores, which has pioneered a focus the company itself characterizes as "upscale discount." Target's activities provide a blueprint for other merchants; the company has commissioned esteemed brands like Calphalon and Waverly to launch affordable lines of their kitchen and home products for its stores, while recruiting well-known designers—notably Michael Graves and

Philippe Starck—to create exclusive items with a European flavor. The strategy has made Target an everyday shopping phenomenon among well-heeled urbanites and prosperous professionals. The higher a consumer's income bracket, the more likely she is to prefer Target to competitors like Wal-Mart and Kmart. (According to a recent CNN/USA Today Gallup Poll, only 16% of consumers earning $16,000 or less shop at Target, but that percentage grows to 47% among those with annual incomes exceeding $75,000.) Wal-Mart has been responding by cautiously adding items such as fresh herbs, gourmet desserts, digital cameras, and 14-karat (rather than 10-karat) gold jewelry to its stores in upscale suburbs like Plano, Texas, and Alpharetta, Georgia.

Beyond upgrading assortments, some retailers have carved out a spot for their more affluent customers—literally—by creating stores within stores. An example is Sears's decision to partner with Dell by placing kiosks in its stores, clearly branded and distinct from the store's more general areas. Sears has also introduced its recently acquired clothing line Lands' End as a form of in-store boutique.

But perhaps the most effective strategy for serving affluent customers is to give them entire stores or malls of their own. If you've been to one of the "lifestyle centers" built by developers Poag & McEwen, you've had a taste of this concept. These complexes feature open-air shopping, high-end stores, and parking lot access to every shop. And because they are small compared with typical malls, they can be located closer to affluent neighborhoods. Aesthetically, too, they are a far cry from the walled retail fortresses often found in suburban hubs. Sophisticated landscaping and architecture lend more of a Main Street quality to the centers. Most appealing to customers is the attitudinal shift these complexes imply; they reject the notion of a shopping center as a destination in itself. The strategy is not to lure the masses out to the hinterlands for a shopping extravaganza—the Mall of America in Minneapolis being a good example of this—but to serve the masses locally in familiar surroundings. As a result, lifestyle center customers average five visits per month as compared with three for the mall, and they spend 50% more per visit. With stores like Williams-Sonoma, Pottery Barn, and Coldwater Creek, but no anchor stores, and a variety of restaurants, spas, and salons, Poag & McEwen's centers earn an average of $397 per square foot (with some earning up to $500) while regional malls earn less than $300.

Reaching the mass market is about having the right retail channels, as we've said. But it's even more famously about promotion—the sloganeering, media buying, and couponing that drum up demand. And, in an era when marketing and technology have drilled down to the level of individual customers, this is the aspect of mass marketing considered most passé. Conventional wisdom says it simply isn't possible to communicate a message to everyone, let alone cost-effectively. As media have splintered and proliferated, and consumers have gained sophistication (both technical and psychological) in blocking out advertising, we've seen the rise of direct marketing, interactive marketing, even permission marketing. Is it possible to contemplate "mass" promotion to an affluent customer base?

The answer is yes, but the promotion schemes must be better suited to the realities of the lives of the moneyed masses. One company that hits them where they live is Captivate Network. It equips elevators in office high-rises with flat-panel TV screens and sells advertising spots, which it mixes in with programming (news headlines and weather forecasts, for instance) from major media-company partners. Given people's tendency to avoid eye contact in elevators, and the very low likelihood of their pulling out reading material, the ads become an almost welcome—and certainly inescapable—diversion. Not only is the demographic spot-on for targeting mass affluence, the ads are wonderfully timed; they reach consumers when they are up and moving, not hunkered down at home wanting only a well-earned rest.

This is just one of the mass promotion techniques we found particularly apropos for the moneyed masses. We've seen companies successfully retool traditional mass-advertising and promotion methods by creatively altering where the sale is situated, who is involved in the selling, and what is given as an incentive. Johnnie Walker, for example, hosts blended whiskey tastings for select groups of consumers. It's an effective strategy given the marketing challenge they faced as single-malt Scotches gained a broader following. Advertising might not have convinced anyone that a blended whiskey could in fact be superior to a single malt—but the company's experts, further credentialed by their rich Scottish accents, could make the point to a group of influencers and get something of a buzz going.

The Trickle-Up Effect

In this article, we've made many suggestions for marketing to today's more moneyed consumers. We've highlighted the emergence of a new consumer market, which, by virtue of being "mass" and also affluent, constitutes the biggest growth opportunity out there for many companies. And we've drawn lessons from the companies that have experimented with new strategies and been successful.

Are we completely comfortable with urging marketers to start mining this vein? Is there any honor in teaching companies not to leave money on the table? If more of the world's nearly rich and merely rich are caused to part with more of their discretionary income, is that a good thing?

Yes, yes, and yes. And if we had any doubts on that score, we were reassured by new research coming out of Northwestern University. Kiminori Matsuyama, an economist there, recently published a fascinating analysis of the effects of income distributions on mass consumption in developed societies. His work shows that two virtuous cycles are in effect in mass consumption. The first is a trickle-down effect, whereby price decreases (from increased productivity, learning-curve improvements, and scale efficiencies) lead to increased demand and consumer access at ever-decreasing levels of income. DVD players, for instance, have gone from $199 to $39— easily accessible now to most any consumer.

But there is also a trickle-up effect that is equally important to the health of an economy. "Trickle up" refers to the fact that, as prices of goods drop, the richer consumers who once spent more to buy those goods end up experiencing, in effect, a bonus in the form of dollars freed up to be spent elsewhere. More dollars in their pockets means they can reach to a higher price point for some other desired good they could not otherwise afford. And more buyers in those categories, in turn, lead to increased competition and innovation there, pushing prices down, renewing the whole cycle once again.

The trickle up of spare dollars, therefore, fuels an explosive expansion of the economy. But that's only the case, Matsuyama theorizes, if income is distributed in a certain way, as it is now. Without the kind of attenuated slope seen in the exhibit "The Emergence of Mass Affluence," gaps appear in the sequence, and the dominoes don't fall. Isolated markets can form at the top and bottom of the income range, and innovation is prevented from flowing across markets. The smoother and more continuous the range of incomes in a mass consumption economy, the smoother the flow of innovation down to the lowest earners. Matsuyama says, "Income distribution should be neither too equal nor too unequal. If it is too equal, the process [of innovation and consumption flow] does not begin. If it is too unequal, it stops prematurely."

When everybody participates in the flow of innovation, everybody stands to benefit. When some people are shut out or opt out, the whole system suffers. Right now, we've got a mass of people representing 49% of the nation's income but only 37% of its consumption. Time to get them back in the pool.

Originally published in July–August 2004
Reprint R0407G

When to Ally and When to Acquire

JEFFREY H. DYER, PRASHANT KALE, AND
HARBIR SINGH

Executive Summary

ACQUISITIONS AND ALLIANCES are two pillars of
growth strategy. But most businesses don't treat the two
as alternative mechanisms for attaining goals. Consequently, companies take over firms they should have collaborated with, and vice versa, and make a mess of both
acquisitions and alliances.

It's easy to see why companies don't weigh the relative merits and demerits of acquisitions and alliances
before choosing horses for courses. The two strategies
differ in many ways: Acquisition deals are competitive,
based on market prices, and risky; alliances are cooperative, negotiated, and not so risky. Companies habitually
deploy acquisitions to increase scale or cut costs and
use partnerships to enter new markets, customer segments, and regions. Moreover, a company's initial experiences often turn into blinders. If the firm pulls off an

alliance or two, it tends to enter into alliances even when circumstances demand acquisitions. Organizational barriers also stand in the way. In many companies, an M&A group, which reports to the finance head, handles acquisitions, while a separate business development unit looks after alliances. The two teams work out of different locations, jealously guard turf, and in effect, prevent companies from comparing the advantages and disadvantages of the strategies.

But companies could improve their results, the authors argue, if they compared the two strategies to determine which is best suited to the situation at hand. Firms such as Cisco that use acquisitions and alliances appropriately grow faster than rivals do. The authors provide a framework to help organizations systematically decide between acquisition and alliance by analyzing three sets of factors: the resources and synergies they desire, the marketplace they compete in, and their competencies at collaborating.

AT THE CORE OF YOUR company's strategy lies a dilemma, wrapped in a problem, inside a challenge. As companies find it increasingly tougher to achieve and sustain growth, they have placed their faith in acquisitions and alliances to boost sales, profits, and, importantly, stock prices. That's most evident in developed countries. American companies, for instance, created a titanic acquisitions and alliances wave by announcing 74,000 acquisitions and 57,000 alliances from 1996 through 2001. During those six years, CEOs signed, roughly, an acquisition and a partnership every hour each day and drove up the acquisitions' combined value to $12 trillion. The pace of collaboration has slowed since then. U.S. firms struck only 7,795 acquisitions and 5,048 alliances in 2002 as compared with 12,460 and 10,349, respectively, in 2000, according to data from Thomson Financial. But as companies gear up for greater growth, collaboration is once again high on priority lists. In fact, firms clinched more acquisition deals (8,385) and alliance agreements (5,789) in 2003 than in the previous year.

There's a problem, however, and it refuses to go away. Most acquisitions and alliances fail. A few may succeed, but acquisitions, on average, either destroy or don't add shareholder value, and alliances typically create very little wealth for shareholders. Companies' share prices fall by between 0.34% and 1% in the ten days after they announce acquisitions, according to three recent studies in the *Strategic Management Journal*. (The target companies' stock prices rise by 30%, on average, implying that their shareholders take home most of the value.) Unlike wines, acquisitions don't get better over time. Acquiring firms experience a wealth loss of 10% over five years after the merger completion, according to a study in the *Journal of Finance*. To add to CEOs' woes, research suggests that 40% to 55% of alliances break down prematurely and inflict financial damage on both partners. When we analyzed 1,592 alliances that 200 U.S. companies had formed between 1993 and 1997, we too found that 48% ended in failure in less than 24 months. There's plenty of evidence: Be it the DaimlerChrysler merger or the Disney and Pixar alliance, collaborations often make headlines for the wrong reasons. Clearly, companies still don't cope very well with either acquisitions or alliances.

What *are* we missing? For more than three decades, academics and consultants have studied acquisitions and alliances and written more tomes on those topics than on virtually any other subject. They've applied everything from game theory to behavioral science to help companies "master" acquisitions and "win" at alliances. They've worshipped at the altars of firms that got the stray acquisition or alliance right.

Surprisingly, although executives instinctively talk about acquisitions and alliances in the same breath, few treat them as alternative mechanisms by which companies can attain goals. We've studied acquisitions and alliances for 20 years and tracked several over time, from announcement to amalgamation or annulment. Our research shows that most companies simply don't compare the two strategies before picking one (see the exhibit "Practicing Versus Preaching"). Consequently, they take over firms they should have collaborated with and ally with those they should have bought, making a mess of both acquisitions and alliances.

It isn't difficult to see why companies don't weigh the merits and demerits of acquisitions and alliances before

---

Practicing Versus Preaching

We conducted a survey of 200 U.S. companies in 2002 to find out what executives said about acquisitions and alliances—and what they actually did.

Do you view acquisitions and alliances as two different ways of achieving the same growth goals?	**82%** Yes	**18%** No
When your company executed its last acquisition, did it consider the alternative of forming an alliance (or continuing the alliance, if it already had one)?	**24%** Yes	**76%** No
Has your company developed any specific policy guidelines or criteria for choosing between forming an alliance with and acquiring a potential partner?	**14%** Yes	**86%** No

choosing horses for courses. The two strategies differ in many ways. Acquisition deals are competitive, based on market prices, and risky; alliances are cooperative, negotiated, and not so risky. So companies habitually deploy acquisitions to increase scale or cut costs and use partnerships to enter new markets, customer segments, and regions. Moreover, a company's initial experiences often turn into blinders. If the firm pulls off an alliance or two, it will forever insist on entering into alliances even when circumstances demand acquisitions. Organizational barriers also stand in the way. In many companies, an M&A group, which reports to the finance head, handles acquisitions, while a separate unit, headed by the business development director or VP, looks after alliances. The two teams work out of different locations, jealously guard turf, and, in effect, prevent companies from comparing the advantages and disadvantages of the strategies.

Some of the world's most admired companies haven't developed a sophisticated enough understanding of when to acquire or ally with other firms. For instance, Coca-Cola and Procter & Gamble announced in February 2001 that they would create a $4 billion joint venture that would control 40-plus brands and employ more than 10,000 people. Coke would transfer Minute Maid, Five Alive, Fruitopia, Cappy, Kapo, Sonfil, and Qoo brands, among others, to the new company, and P&G would contribute two beverage brands, Sunny Delight and Punica, and Pringles chips. Coke would tap P&G's expertise in nutrition to develop new drinks, P&G's flagging brands would get a boost from Coke's international distribution system, and the new company would slash costs by $50 million, ran the prepared script. Yet Coke's stock dropped by 6% the day the alliance was announced, while P&G's shares rose by 2%. Investors wondered why Coke had agreed to share 50% of the profits from a fast-growing segment with a weak rival in its core business. The unspoken question: If Coke needed P&G's soft-drink technologies and brands, why hadn't it simply bought them? It wasn't long before the companies wondered the same thing; Coke and P&G terminated the alliance in July 2001.

Another case in point is Intel, which paid $1.6 billion in cash in October 1999 to buy the $131 million DSP Communications, which manufactures chips for wireless handsets. Although the acquisition allowed Intel to break into the wireless communications market, its stock price fell by 11% over three days after the deal was made. Investors were concerned about the 40% premium that Intel paid for DSP's shares. In addition, people tend to leave high-tech firms when bigger companies absorb them, and technologies get obsolete quickly. Those factors usually trigger post-acquisition trauma. Sure enough, Intel lost most of DSP's key people and its biggest wireless customer, Kyocera, when it absorbed the start-up. Intel had to write off $600 million of goodwill by 2003. Should the company have tested the airwaves by initially entering into an alliance with DSP?

Such questions needn't be answered only with the wisdom of hindsight. We've developed a framework that will help companies systematically decide whether they should ally with or acquire potential partners. Our research shows that executives must analyze three sets of factors before deciding on a collaboration option: the resources and synergies they desire, the marketplace they compete in, and their competencies at collaborating. Of course, companies must develop the ability to execute both acquisitions and alliances if they want to grow. Knowing when to use which strategy may, however, be a greater source of competitive advantage than knowing how to execute them.

Resources and Synergies

It's the most abused concept in the acquisitions and alliances dictionary, but companies team up to profit from the synergies they can generate by combining resources. Firms bring many kinds of resources to the table: human resources (intellectual capital, for instance); intangibles (like brand names); technological resources (such as patents); physical resources (plants, distribution networks, and so forth); and, of course, financial resources. Whenever companies have to choose between acquisitions and alliances, they must begin the process by examining key resource-related issues.

TYPES OF SYNERGIES

Companies create three kinds of synergies by combining and customizing resources differently. Those resource combinations, or interdependencies, as we call them, require different levels of coordination between firms and result in different forms of collaboration.

First, companies create *modular synergies* when they manage resources independently and pool only the results for greater profits. (The synergies are modular because modularly interdependent resources generate them.) When an airline and a hotel chain plan a collaboration that will allow hotel guests to earn frequent flyer miles, they wish to club the consumer's choice of airline and hotel, so that both benefit from her decision. Companies will find that nonequity alliances are usually best suited to generate modular synergies. For instance, like other companies in the information technology industry, Hewlett-Packard and Microsoft have created a nonequity alliance that pools the companies' systems integration and enterprise software skills, respectively, to create technology solutions for small and big customers.

Second, firms derive *sequential synergies* when one company completes its tasks and passes on the results to a partner to do its bit. In those cases, the resources of the two firms are sequentially interdependent. For instance, when a biotech firm that specializes in discovering new drugs, like Abgenix, wishes to work with a pharmaceutical giant that is more familiar with the FDA approvals process, such as AstraZeneca, both companies are seeking sequential synergies. Companies must customize resources to some extent if they want handoffs between the organizations to go smoothly. According to our research, that will likely happen only if partners sign rigid contracts that they monitor very carefully, or better, enter into equity-based alliances.

Third, companies generate *reciprocal synergies* by working closely together and executing tasks through an iterative knowledge-sharing process. Not only do firms have to combine resources, but they have to customize them a great deal to make them reciprocally interdependent. For companies that desire those synergies, acquisitions are better than alliances. In the mid-1990s, for instance, Exxon and Mobil realized that they would have to become more efficient in almost every part of the value chain, from research and oil exploration to marketing and distribution, in order to remain competitive. The two giants could do that only by combining all assets and functions, and so they merged in 1999 rather than pursuing an alliance.

NATURE OF RESOURCES

Before settling on a strategy, companies should check if they must create the synergies they desire by combining hard resources, like manufacturing plants, or soft resources, such as people. When the synergy-generating resources are hard, acquisitions are a better option. That's because hard assets are easy to value, and companies can generate synergies from them relatively quickly. Take the case of Masco Corporation, which has grown its home improvement products business by acquiring 150 companies in the past 40 years, 20 of them between 2000 and 2002. After every acquisition, Masco quickly scales up the acquired firm's manufacturing capacity to generate economies of scale, combines the companies' raw materials purchases, and merges distribution networks. By repeatedly using that three-pronged process, Masco has stayed profitable over the years.

When companies have to generate synergies by combining human resources, it's a good idea to avoid acquisitions. Research suggests that employees of acquired companies become unproductive because they are disinclined to work in the predator's interests and believe that they have lost freedom. In fact, people often walk out the door after acquisitions. Two studies show that acquirers of companies that had largely soft assets lost more value over a three-year period than did buyers of businesses with mostly hard assets. There's no dearth of examples. When NationsBank (now Bank-America) picked up Montgomery Securities in 1997, the integration process didn't account for the cultural and compensation differ-

ences between commercial and investment banks. Key
employees headed for the door, and Bank-America never
benefited from the acquisition.

Not surprisingly, equity alliances may be a better bet
than acquisitions in collaborations that involve people.
An equity stake allows companies to control the actions
of their partners, monitor performance better, and align
the interests of the two firms more closely. At the same
time, the arrangement avoids the disaffection and mass
exodus of employees associated with takeovers. Of
course, firms will find it easier to achieve synergies if they
can persuade their corporate partners to sell some shares
to their key employees. Both the organization and people
will then be committed to common goals.

EXTENT OF REDUNDANT RESOURCES

Companies must estimate the amount of redundant
resources they'll be saddled with if they team up with
other organizations. They can use the surplus resources
to generate economies of scale, or they can cut costs by
eliminating those resources. When companies have a
large amount of redundant resources, they should opt for
acquisitions or mergers. That gives executives complete
control over decision making and allows them to get rid
of redundant resources easily. One of the key drivers of
the Hewlett-Packard and Compaq merger, for instance,
was resource redundancy. HP and Compaq claimed that
they could eliminate redundancies across the value
chain, all the way from administration, procurement,
and manufacturing to product development and marketing. Their aim was to generate $2 billion of savings in fis-
cal 2003, and even more in later years. HP and Compaq

would not have been able to achieve those results with the most comprehensive of alliances.

To sum up, when companies want reciprocal synergies or have large quantities of redundant resources, whether the assets are hard or soft, they must think in terms of acquisitions. At the other end of the spectrum, when businesses desire synergies from sequential interdependence and are combining mostly soft assets, equity alliances may be the best bet. When companies want to generate modular or sequential synergies, and the assets that will create them are mostly hard, like factories, they can choose contractual alliances. For instance, Toys R Us knows how to spot hot toys, while Amazon uses online selling and order-fulfillment skills to sell them to customers. Because the duo wanted to generate sequential synergies with hard assets, a contractual alliance between Toys R Us and Amazon has worked well for both companies. See the exhibit "Choosing Between Acquisitions and Alliances" for further information.

Market Factors

Many companies believe that collaboration decisions are internal matters. They don't take into account external factors before picking strategies—and invariably fall victim to market forces. Companies should consider exogenous factors, like market uncertainty and competition, even if they can't control them.

DEGREES OF UNCERTAINTY

Executives know that collaborations between companies are inherently risky, but don't realize that they've

Choosing Between Acquisitions and Alliances

When pursuing collaboration as a growth strategy, managers must carefully analyze several key factors before deciding whether to acquire or to ally with a company. Once they've determined what kind of resources they plan to combine, the types of synergies they're hoping to create, and the market and competitive factors they face, managers can use this framework to choose the strategic option best suited to their situation. Managers should weigh each factor depending on its importance to their industry. In all cases, the collaboration competencies a company already possesses should be considered in making a decision.

Factor	Strategy
1. Types of Synergies	
Modular	Nonequity alliances
Sequential	Equity alliances
Reciprocal	Acquisitions
2. Nature of Resources	
Relative value of soft to hard resources	
Low	Nonequity alliances
Low/Medium	Acquisitions
High	Equity alliances
3. Extent of Redundant Resources	
Low	Nonequity alliances
Medium	Equity alliances
High	Acquisitions
4. Degree of Market Uncertainty	
Low	Nonequity alliances
Low/Medium	Acquisitions
High	Equity alliances
5. Level of Competition	
Degree of competition for resources	
Low	Nonequity alliances
Medium	Equity alliances
High	Acquisitions

become downright uncertain in a fast-changing world. Risk exists when companies can assess the probability distribution of future payoffs; the wider the distribution, the higher the risk. Uncertainty exists when it isn't possible to assess future payoffs. Companies are forced to decide how to team up with other firms, especially small ones, without knowing whether there will be payoffs, what they might be, and when the benefits might come their way.

Before entering into an acquisition or alliance, companies should break down the uncertainty that surrounds the collaboration's outcome into two components. First, managers must evaluate the uncertainty associated with the technology or product it is discussing with the potential partner. Can we tell if the widget will work? Is it technically superior to existing and potential rivals? Second, the company should assess if consumers will use the technology, product, or service and how much time it will take to gain widespread acceptance. Based on the answers—or lack thereof—the company can estimate if the degree of uncertainty that clouds the collaboration's end result is low, high, or somewhere in between.

When a company estimates that a collaboration's outcome is highly or moderately uncertain, it should enter into a nonequity or equity alliance rather than acquire the would-be partner. An alliance will limit the firm's exposure since it has to invest less money and time than it would in an acquisition. Besides, the company can sink more into the partnership if it starts showing results, and, if necessary, buy the firm eventually. If the collaboration doesn't yield results, the company can withdraw from the alliance. It may lose money and prestige, but that will be nowhere near the costs of a failed acquisition.

That isn't exactly rocket science, but our research shows that few companies are disciplined enough to adhere to those rules. For instance, Hoffmann-La Roche spent $2.1 billion in June 1999 to acquire Genentech, which had developed a clot-busting drug, TPA, but hadn't completed effectiveness studies or sought FDA approval. Roche thought it could help the start-up get clearances for the drug quickly and then push it through its global distribution network. Six months later, a study found that TPA, which Roche had priced at $2,200 per dose, was only as effective at clearing clots as Hoechst's streptokinase, which sold at $200 a dose. That dashed Roche's hopes. TPA grew into a respectable $200-million-per-annum drug, but it never became the blockbuster Roche paid for. Given the high technical uncertainty in the drug development process, Roche should not have bought Genentech.

Not every company makes such mistakes. Bristol-Myers Squibb invested $1 billion to pick up a 20% equity stake in ImClone in September 2001 rather than buying the firm. In return, it bagged the marketing rights to ImClone's cancer-fighting drug, Erbitux, as well as 40% of annual profits. According to the deal, Bristol-Myers Squibb would invest $800 million more after ImClone got past key milestones in the drug approval process. In December 2001, when the FDA declined to review Erbitux due to "severely deficient" data, ImClone's share price plunged from over $60 to $25 within two weeks (and shook up offices on Wall Street and suburban homes in the U.S. in the process). The companies immediately renegotiated the alliance, and the giant will invest less in ImClone in the future. Had it chosen to acquire ImClone for the asking price of $5 billion, rather than allying with it, Bristol-Myers Squibb would have been gazing out of a $3.5 billion hole in its books instead of a $650 million one.

FORCES OF COMPETITION

There's a well-developed market for M&A in the world, so companies would be wise to check if they have rivals for potential partners before pursuing a deal. If there are several suitors, a company may have no choice but to buy a firm in order to preempt the competition. Still, companies should avoid taking over other firms when the degree of business uncertainty is very high. Instead, the company should negotiate an alliance that will let it pick up a majority stake at a future date after some of the uncertainty has receded.

Take, for instance, the manner in which Pfizer used an alliance with Warner-Lambert as a gateway to an acquisition. In June 1996, Pfizer offered to collaborate in the marketing of Lipitor, a new cholesterol-reducing drug that Warner-Lambert had developed. Lipitor was technically superior to competing products in some ways, but it was a late entrant in the market. Doctors and consumers were used to four other products in that category, and it wasn't clear if they would accept Lipitor immediately. Given the high technological and market uncertainty, Pfizer rightly believed that a contractual alliance made the most sense. Partly due to Pfizer's marketing acumen and distribution system, Lipitor's sales crossed $1 billion in its very first year, and by 1999, it had become a blockbuster drug with an annual turnover of $3 billion.

Even as Pfizer was exploring the possibility of working more closely with Warner-Lambert, archrival American Home Products and Warner-Lambert announced a surprise $72 billion merger in November 1999. The next day, Pfizer made an $80 billion counteroffer for its partner. Procter & Gamble jumped into the fray with a plan to acquire both AHP and Warner-Lambert but withdrew after investors reacted angrily. The battle between AHP and Pfizer for Warner-Lambert raged on for weeks, but it was a foregone conclusion. Pfizer's alliance with Warner-Lambert to market Lipitor, the cost-cutting opportunities it had spotted, and the possibility that Pfizer could combine one of its drugs, Norvasc, with Lipitor together gave Pfizer a distinct edge over American Home Products. By February 2000, Pfizer had won the battle for Warner-Lambert with a $100 billion bid.

Collaboration Capabilities

A company's experience in managing acquisitions or alliances is bound to influence its choices. Some businesses have developed abilities to manage acquisitions or alliances over the years and regard them as core competencies. They've created special teams to act as repositories of knowledge and institutionalized processes to identify targets, bid or negotiate with them, handle due diligence, and tackle issues that arise after a deal is made. They've learned the dos and don'ts from experience and created templates that help executives manage specific acquisition- or alliance-related tasks. In addition, they've developed formal and informal training programs that sharpen managers' deal-related skills. GE Capital, Symantec, and Bank One, among others, have created acquisition competencies, while Hewlett-Packard, Siebel, and Eli Lilly, for example, have systematically built alliance capabilities.

It's tempting to say that companies should use the strategy that they are good at because it does improve their chances of making collaborations work. However, specialization poses a problem because companies with hammers tend to see everything as nails. Since most firms have developed either alliance or acquisition skills, they often become committed to what they're good at. They stick to pet strategies even if they aren't appropriate and make poor choices.

Smart companies prevent such mistakes by developing skills to handle both acquisitions and alliances. That isn't as easy as it sounds. Take Corning. For decades, it had cultivated the ability to manage alliances. In the 1990s, however, the company used acquisitions to expand in the telecommunications business. Corning faced several challenges and much criticism because it had little experience in handling takeovers. While Corning made many mistakes, the company may have been on the right track when it tried not to let habit determine its choices. In fact, our research shows that companies that use both acquisitions and alliances grow faster than rivals do—as companies like Cisco have amply demonstrated.

How Cisco Does It

Everyone knows that Cisco follows an acquisitions-led growth strategy. The networking giant has acquired and successfully absorbed 36 firms in the last ten years. What most people don't realize, however, is that Cisco entered into more than 100 alliances in the same period—and managed them well. Largely because of Cisco's dual growth strategy, between 1993 and 2003, the company's sales and market capitalization grew by an average of 36% and 44%, respectively, every year. Just how does Cisco succeed where almost every other company fails?

A key reason is that Cisco has one senior vice president in charge of corporate development, who is responsible for M&A, strategic alliances, and technology incubation. By placing all three functions under the same person, Cisco is able to look internally first, and then, if there are no viable options for meeting its objectives, consider either an alliance or an acquisition. Dan Scheinman, Cisco's head of corporate development, told us, "This is where we make the choice between internal development, acquisitions, or alliances. At some point, I have to make the decision about what's the right strategy for us." Each time, Scheinman makes the call with the help of two vice presidents in charge of M&A and alliances.

The VPs head teams that have honed the ability to execute acquisitions and alliances. Usually, Cisco will first assess whether a target company has a technology that is critical to Cisco's core products. The target company's technology, when combined with Cisco's technologies, must provide solutions that customers will demand immediately and in the future. If that seems likely, Cisco will acquire the business right away. However, the $18 billion giant believes that it can absorb other firms' technologies only if their facilities and people are located nearby. Cisco avoids deals that would require employees to relocate because they usually leave the company instead of moving. Thus, Cisco rarely buys companies that are not located in its general neighborhood.

When there is a high degree of uncertainty around technologies, or when they aren't critical, Cisco uses alliances as stepping-stones to acquisitions. Approximately 25% of Cisco's acquisitions start as small equity investments. That allows Cisco to get some partners to accelerate development of products, take options on competing technologies, and evaluate firms to determine if acquisitions will work. According to the company, it takes between 12 and 18 months to build trust with partners and decide if the companies can work together. The equity relationships also help Cisco move quickly to preempt rivals and acquire firms when the time is right. Clearly, Cisco has used both acquisitions and alliances successfully because it has developed processes that help it determine when to use which strategy.

• • •

To conclude, let us return to the beginning and two deals, Coke's alliance with P&G and Intel's acquisition of DSP Communications. Would these companies have done any better by using our framework? In the case of Coke and P&G, the companies had plenty of redundant resources and wanted to generate reciprocal synergies primarily from hard resources. According to our framework, acquisitions are most appropriate under those circumstances. Next, market uncertainty was relatively low for the venture's products, but competition would have been high. Once again, the framework suggests that when rivalry is intense but uncertainty is low, acquisitions are the best bet. Coke should have acquired P&G's health drinks business instead of entering into a joint venture.

Although Intel took over DSP, the two companies wanted to generate modular synergies since the degree of resource interdependence between Intel's microprocessors and DSP's wireless chips businesses would have been moderate. Moreover, DSP's resources appeared to be primarily people. Whenever soft resources are involved, according to our framework, a red flag should go up about the appropriateness of acquisitions. Besides, Intel and DSP had little resource redundancy, and wireless technologies are highly uncertain. Those factors also suggest that an equity-based alliance between Intel and DSP, which Intel could have used as a springboard to an acquisition, would have been more effective than acquisition. As the mathematician would say, QED.

Originally published in July–August 2004
Reprint R0407H

Getting the Most out of All Your Customers

JACQUELYN S. THOMAS, WERNER
REINARTZ, AND V. KUMAR

Executive Summary

COMPANIES SPEND BILLIONS OF DOLLARS on direct
marketing, targeting individual customers with ever more
accuracy. Yet despite the power of the myriad data-
collecting and analytical tools at their disposal, they're
still having trouble optimizing their direct-marketing
investments.

Many marketers try to minimize costs by pursuing
only those customers who are cheap to find and cheap
to keep. Others try to get the most customers they possibly can and keep all of them for as long as they can. But
a customer need not be loyal to be highly profitable,
and many loyal customers turn out to be highly unprofitable. Companies can get more out of direct marketing
if they see it as a single system for generating profits than
if they try to maximize performance measures at each

stage of the process. This article describes a tool for doing just that.

Called ARPRO (Allocating Resources for Profits), the tool is essentially a complex regression analysis that can estimate the impact of a company's direct-marketing investments on the profitability of its customer pool. With data that companies already gather, the tool can show managers how much to spend on acquisition versus retention and even what percentage of their funds they should allocate to the different direct-marketing channels.

Using the model, companies can easily see that even small deviations from the optimal levels of customer profitability are expensive. Applying it to one catalog retailer showed, for instance, that a 10% reduction in marketing costs would lead to a $1.8 million drop in long-term customer profits. Conversely, spending 69% less on marketing would actually increase average customer profitability at one B2B service provider by 42%. What's more, the tool can show that finding the optimal balance between investments in acquisition and retention can be more important than finding the optimum amount to invest overall.

COMPANIES SPEND BILLIONS OF DOLLARS every year marketing directly to potential customers and managing relationships with existing ones. Increasingly, thanks to technologies allowing them to gather extraordinarily rich data on consumer demographics and behavior, firms can make the individual the principal unit of analysis and management. Armed with these data, they can tailor their messages—targeting just those people who would be likely to want a particular product or suggesting additional items that current customers would be likely to buy. At the same time, using related technologies that allow them to reach consumers through many different channels, companies can improve the overall effectiveness of their marketing communications, further increasing their potential profits.

Over the last decade, firms in sectors as diverse as retailing, pharmaceuticals, and business-to-business services have increased the scale and pace of their direct marketing and developed an arsenal of analytic tools to help them more precisely identify and manage their individual customers: lift and gains charts; response analysis; recency, frequency, and monetary value (RFM) models; decision trees; decision calculus; and many others. The new tools have gone a long way toward improving the effectiveness of marketing investments. Otto Versand of Hamburg, Germany, the largest mail-order company in the world, is an especially sophisticated user; given enough data, it can predict with almost 80% accuracy whether an individual will respond to a particular mailing. This capacity gives the retailer a significant competitive advantage. In 2003, for instance, Otto Versand was able to grow revenues of its North American subsidiary Crate and Barrel (retail and mail-order) by 12.6% to $865 million in a very hostile retail climate. Using its formidable customer-targeting skills in its joint venture with the Spanish fashion retailer Zara, it also grew revenues in the German market a whopping 70%.

Yet despite such successes, our empirical evidence suggests that many companies are still struggling with their direct-marketing investments. In a recent study, we analyzed the marketing budgets of three well-regarded firms. At one, also a catalog retailer, we estimated that a 31% *reduction* in marketing investment per customer would *increase* average customer profitability by about 29%. An annual decrease of 69%, we found at the second company—a business-to-business service provider—would increase average customer profitability by 42%. Conversely, at the third firm, a pharmaceutical giant, we estimated that a 31% increase in annual direct-marketing investment per customer would improve average customer profitability 36%.

Why are these companies so off the mark? In the following pages, we argue that in making direct-marketing investment decisions, too many marketers still overemphasize short-term cost over long-term gain, favoring the pursuit of customers who are cheap to acquire and cheap to retain without necessarily being very profitable. We also raise a more subtle problem: Maximizing customer acquisition and customer retention separately does not maximize profits. As with any supply chain, companies can get more out of direct marketing if they see it as a single system for generating profits than if they try to maximize performance measures at each stage of the process.

There are some technical difficulties involved, however, because the data companies rely on to estimate the potential profitability of their customer pools are skewed toward the customers they already have. We will present a tool that gets around this problem and allows managers to take an integrated approach to deciding how much and where to spend their companies' marketing dollars and efforts. Using data that companies already gather, the tool can guide managers in deciding how much to spend on direct marketing, what percentages they should devote to acquisition versus retention, and even what percentage of their funds they should allocate to the different direct-marketing channels to get the most profits from each customer. We'll demonstrate how powerful that information can be by applying the tool to the three companies we've studied in depth.

Where Companies Go Wrong

In our experience, most companies still use the customer acquisition rate (the percentage of people targeted by a direct-marketing effort who actually become customers) and the customer retention rate (the duration of a customer's relationship with the firm) as their principal metrics of marketing performance. That's partly because these variables are easy to understand and track and partly because companies have long had an obsession with market share. And for some businesses, of course, they are very accurate proxies for performance—subscriber-based magazines are a case in point.

But for a great many industries, using acquisition and retention rates as measures of overall performance is highly problematic for a variety of reasons. First and most obvious, focusing on raising rates ever higher encourages marketers to overlook the law of diminishing returns. Inevitably, beyond a certain point, the cost of acquiring or retaining a customer outweighs the revenues he or she will bring in; after that point, of course, increasing the acquisition or retention rate only lowers the company's profitability. And yet, we're constantly surprised by how often marketing departments treat cost-effectiveness as an afterthought.

Many companies alert to this first trap run into a second. Typically, we've found that their managers focus too much on the present cost of acquiring and retaining customers and not enough on their customers' long-term value. Indeed, many marketers explicitly or implicitly group their customers into four segments, solely according to the difficulty and cost of acquiring and retaining them, essentially ignoring the revenues those individuals generate. The first group contains the people who are easy to acquire and easy to retain. The second comprises those who are difficult to acquire but easy to maintain. In the third group are the people who are easy to acquire but hard to retain, and the fourth group holds those who are difficult both to acquire and to maintain. The consequences of this approach are obvious: If both sales staff and relationship managers are targeting the people who are easiest to please, the company will end up with a disproportionate number of customers who are both easy to acquire and easy to retain. Modern technology makes this all the more likely to happen, as it enables marketers to identify precisely who those individuals are.

That would not be a problem if all customers were equally profitable or if acquisition and retention costs were overwhelmingly the major determinants of customer profitability. But a look at the numbers shows otherwise, as we found when we studied detailed customer data provided by the catalog retailer.

We tracked the behavior over three years of a single cohort of customers who all began their relationships with the firm in the same quarter. We determined which group each customer fell into, how much was spent to acquire and retain each one, and what contribution each made to the company's profits. When segmenting customers into the four groups, we set the dividing line between "low" and "high" at the median for both the cost of acquisition and the cost of retention (see the exhibit "Does Cost Drive Profits?").

As we expected, the largest segment—32%—was made up of customers who were easy to acquire and retain. But they accounted for only 20% of the entire cohort's profits. The largest profit contribution came from the smallest group, the customers who were expensive to acquire but cheap to retain. They made up only 15% of the total but were responsible for fully 40% of the profits. The next largest contributors to profits—25% of the total—were the seemingly troublesome 28% of the cohort who were both difficult to acquire and difficult to retain. The least profitable customers were the ones who were easy to acquire but then turned out to be difficult to maintain. About 25% of all customers fell into that category, yet collectively they yielded only 15% of the profits.

Does Cost Drive Profits?

Just because customers are cheap to find doesn't mean they're profitable. That's what this mail-order company found when it related the profits its customers generated to the cost and effort it took to acquire and retain them.

	High-maintenance customers	**Royal customers**
High	25% of customers 15% of profits	28% of customers 25% of profits
Retention cost	**Casual customers**	**Low-maintenance customers**
Low	32% of customers 20% of profits	15% of customers 40% of profits
	Low Acquisition cost High	

These findings are not unique to this company; for nearly any firm, profitable customers will be found in all four segments, though the distribution of profits and customers will vary.

Clearly, companies that focus only on customers who are easy to acquire and retain are not allocating their resources as efficiently as they might. The cost and effort of acquisition and retention is just one of many factors they need to consider. And it's not as if reliable data do not exist on the other variables. In fact, the body of customer data is now so rich that managers can—as those at companies like Otto Versand are starting to do—make accurate forecasts of the potential loyalty and potential profitability of any customer and allocate acquisition and retention resources accordingly.

Many companies wise enough to avoid that second trap often fall prey to the third, more subtle trap—treating acquisition and retention as independent activities and trying to maximize both rates. If their marketing budgets are not constrained by other factors, such companies will almost certainly find themselves overinvesting in both activities. In trying to acquire the most possible customers, they will attract some who are not profitable but remain stubbornly loyal and, conversely, others who while highly profitable in an instance or two will never be loyal. If retention efforts simply focus on keeping the most customers, companies will not only waste money trying to retain the loyal unprofitable group but will also vainly throw money after the profitable transient group. What's worse, those funds won't be spent on attracting potentially highly profitable customers who are hard to acquire.

Plainly, then, it's a good idea to integrate the management of customer acquisition, customer retention, and

profitability. However, one final—and seemingly insur-
mountable—technical problem stands in the way. In
nearly every case, the models that even the sophisticated
direct marketers use to link customer profitability to
direct-marketing investments are subject to a failing
known to statisticians as selection bias.

Selection bias arises when researchers use a sample
that is not truly representative of the whole population.
If a sample is biased, any relationships inferred from it
can be misleading. In the marketing context, for
instance, selection bias can cause analysts to incorrectly
predict the impact of marketing activities or customer
characteristics on customer behavior, which can lead to
bad marketing investment decisions. And since, to
uncover relationships between customers and profits,
most direct marketers rely heavily on data about actual
customers—who are only a subset of the total pool of
possible customers—they are bound almost by necessity
to estimate the relationship between acquisition, retention, and profits incorrectly. As a result, they will once
again ignore the potential of customers whom they have
not yet succeeded in acquiring or overinvest in the ones
they already have.

Allocating Resources for Profits

To truly manage direct marketing for profits, marketers
need an approach that gets around selection bias so they
can uncover the true relationship between customer
behavior and long-term profits. We believe that our
approach, which we call the ARPRO model (Allocating
Resources for Profits), does just that.

ARPRO is essentially a complex regression analysis in
which, very broadly speaking, total long-term profitability

is a function of factors relating to the amount the company spends on each customer and factors relating to the customer's behavior, with each factor weighted according to its relative importance and the data set adjusted for sample bias.

The challenge in setting up the model, of course, lies in identifying the factors correctly and in accurately determining their relative weightings in the model's various equations. Ideally, these factors should comprise three types of data: what the company does to attract and retain customers, the demographic and psychographic descriptors of the company's customer pool, and the actual buying behavior of those potential customers (how much they buy, how often, what share of wallet, and so on). Certainly, the richer the available information, the better the predictions.

Some of these factors can be directly observed and controlled: the average amounts spent on acquiring customers or on retaining them, for example. Other, more complex and interdependent factors can only be estimated through their own regression analyses. In particular, the average duration of a customer's relationship with the company is partly a function of the amount spent on retention efforts. Once all the elements that make up these factors have been estimated and the weighting coefficients indicating their relative importance have been assigned, managers can manipulate the model by plugging in different amounts for the factors they control to see which values result in optimal customer profitability.

An integrated regression of the factors determining acquisition, retention, and profitability such as we have just described inevitably suffers from the problem of selection bias because it is based on data from retained customers, which are not representative of the whole population of prospective customers. To correct for this bias, we introduce a statistical correction mechanism called lambda, borrowed from Nobel Prize–winning research conducted by University of Chicago economics professor James Heckman to correct sampling biases in unemployment data. Like customer information, unemployment data are riddled with potential selection biases because they're taken only from the ranks of people who choose to work and not from the ones who don't. Thanks to this correction procedure, we can now construct integrated regression models about acquisition, retention, and profitability that eliminate the selection bias arising from data on a company's retained customers.

To illustrate how the ARPRO model works, we'll take a highly simplified hypothetical case in which the total long-term customer profitability for a company is determined only by how much the company spends on acquiring a customer, how much the company invests in retaining a customer, and the duration of the relationship. Even in this simplest of examples, duration is itself a complex factor determined by how much the company invests in retaining its customers. In estimating the relationship between profitability and these three factors for the company's entire population of current and potential customers, however, we also need to account for diminishing returns on our marketing investments over time. So, following standard statistics practice, we subtract the squares of the two investment factors to simulate that effect. Then we add in the lambda factor to correct for selection bias, apply weighting coefficients ($c_1 \ldots c_6$ and $b_1 \ldots b_3$) to all of these factors, and set a starting intercept point. We now have the following two regression equations:

Total long-term customer profitability (dollars) = intercept

$+c_1 \times$ acquisition spending

$-c_2 \times$ (acquisition spending)^2

$+c_3 \times$ retention spending

$-c_4 \times$ (retention spending)^2

$+c_5 \times$ predicted duration

$+c_6 \times$ lambda

Predicted relationship duration (days) = intercept

$+b_1 \times$ retention spending

$- b_2 \times$ (retention spending)^2

$+b_3 \times$ lambda

Our next step is to quantify lambda. The actual math for this calculation is very advanced and beyond the scope of this article, but the data required are not complicated or difficult to acquire. In our experience, the customer information available to most marketing operations—individual-level data on, for example, when each customer came on board, their purchase behavior while each was active, and the kind of marketing aimed not only at existing customers but also at prospects—is more than sufficient for the calculation. (We would refer readers interested in looking at the math to our working paper.[1]) Lambda is always a positive number and can be greater than one. Typically, the higher the average probability of acquiring customers, the smaller the correction factor, reflecting the fact that a greater portion of the potential customers have already been acquired. In our hypothetical case, let's assume that lambda is 0.6. Note also that lambda is a constant as long as we rely on the same basic data.

Next we determine numbers for the weighting factor coefficients, which is done by working out what those relative weights have been in the past, running historical numbers for the various factors in the equation against historical duration and profitability values. For the purposes of this illustration, let's assume that this analysis yields coefficients for our equation as follows:

Total long-term customer profitability (dollars) = 20

+ 5 × acquisition spending

− 0. 25 × (acquisition spending)^2

+ 8 × retention spending

− 0.1 × (retention spending)^2

+ 10 × predicted duration

+ 30 × lambda

Predicted relationship duration (days) = 1

+ 4 × retention spending

− 0.03 × (retention spending)^2

+ 15 × lambda

We are now ready for the final step—seeing what profitability we can predict if we change the levels of investment in acquisition and retention. This is the simplest part of the exercise. All we have to do is systematically plug in different values for retention and acquisition spending into the equations to get alternate customer profitability estimates. After repeating this whole process several times with various amounts, we eventually find the acquisition and retention spending values that optimize customer profitability. In our simulation example for the pharmaceutical company, we used increments of $1, $5, $10, $15, and $20 for acquisition dollars and $40, $50, $60, $70, and $80 for retention dollars. The results of these simulations are summarized in the two tables shown in the exhibit "How Much

Should You Spend?" As the tables show, the optimal spending amounts are $10 on acquiring a customer and $60 on retaining her. Note that investing $60 on retention would not optimize relationship duration, which confirms our belief that retention rates are imperfect predictors of profitability.

What we have presented here is a very simplified model. In practice, we often use a greater number of more precise input variables, including, for instance, the amount of investments in acquisition and retention made in each marketing channel—direct mail, e-mail, and so forth. For a list of the sorts of factors that companies can plug into their equations, see "What Drives Profitability?" at the end of this article. Indeed, the only drawback of this model is that it cannot be used to assess the effectiveness of broadcast advertising, where customer response is impossible to break down by individual. But it is absolutely applicable in any situation where information on individual customer behavior is available and where resources are expended on individual customers, which thanks to modern CRM technology is becoming the dominant approach to marketing in an increasing number of industries.

What We Found

How important is it to optimize spending on direct marketing? Results from our detailed analysis of all three companies demonstrate that even small deviations from the optimal levels of customer profitability are expensive. (You can see the numbers in the exhibit "How Wrong Can You Be?") Let's suppose the catalog retailer, for example, cuts marketing costs by 10%, saving $250,000.

How Much Should You Spend?

Perhaps even more important than spending the optimal total amount on direct marketing is allocating that budget correctly between acquisition and retention efforts. Using our model, you can find the right split. In this example from a pharmaceutical company, we can see, in the first table, the point at which extra spending on customer retention starts to reap diminishing returns. Here, the highest retention rate is achieved with an investment of $70 per customer. But, as the second table shows, the maximum customer profitability occurs when $10 is spent on acquisition and $60 on retention per customer. Thus, the recommended budget split between acquisition and retention is 14% on acquisition (10/70) and 86% on retention (60/70). Together, the tables clearly show that retention and profitability are not altogether mutually reinforcing objectives; optimal allocation decisions derived for each are not necessarily optimal overall.

Average Customer Relationship Duration
(as a function of retention spending)

Retention Spending (per customer)	$40	$50	$60	$70	$80
Estimated Relationship Duration (days)	122	135	142	**143**	138

Average Customer Profitability
(as a function of acquisition and retention spending)

		Retention Spending				
		$40	$50	**$60**	$70	$80
Acquisition Spending	$1	$1,423	$1,543	$1,583	$1,543	$1,423
	$5	$1,437	$1,557	$1,597	$1,557	$1,437
	$10	$1,443	$1,563	**$1,603**	$1,563	$1,443
	$15	$1,437	$1,557	$1,597	$1,557	$1,437
	$20	$1,418	$1,538	$1,578	$1,538	$1,418

The reduction, we estimate, would lead to a 1.2% decrease in profitability per customer. On a base of 60,000 customers, our model indicates that would result in a loss of about $1.8 million in long-term customer profits.

Our findings underline the fact that maximizing the likelihood of acquiring or retaining an individual customer is not the same as maximizing overall customer profitability. By spending more than the optimal amounts we propose, the B2B firm, for example, could indeed increase the likelihood of acquiring a customer (from 22% to 26%) and increase the expected duration of that relationship a bit (from 46 months to 47). Similarly, the pharmaceutical firm, by spending beyond the profit maximization level, could increase the likelihood of acquiring a customer from 24% to 29% and extend duration by four months. But those increases won't translate into optimum profitability.

How Wrong Can You Be?

How much money could a company make if it optimized its direct-marketing expenditures? Here's what we found when we ran the numbers for three companies in three very different fields.

Company	How much more or less should be spent on direct marketing to reach optimal levels.	How much profits would increase if spending on direct marketing were optimal.
B2B	↓ -68.30%	41.52% ↑
Pharmaceutical	31.40% ↑	35.80% ↑
Catalog retailer	↓ -30.70%	28.90% ↑

Yet if spending too much on marketing is bad, spending too little—especially on customer retention—is nearly always worse. If we look only at deviations from the optimal acquisition budget and keep all other factors at their optimum levels, we find that the effects of underspending and overspending are roughly equal for all three firms. But when it comes to customer retention, stinginess is significantly more harmful than extravagance. That's partly because of the correlation between customer profitability and relationship duration: Diminishing returns diminish more swiftly when you overspend on retention than when you underspend.

These differences in the relative impact of retention and acquisition investments complicate the question of finding the right balance when deciding how much to invest in each. Suppose, for instance, that the marketing department of the pharmaceutical firm in our study is ordered to reduce its total direct-marketing and communication budget by 5%. It can do so in several ways. One is to cut its acquisition and retention budgets by 5% each. Another is to cut its acquisition budget by 25%, leaving the retention budget unchanged. Obviously, deviating from the optimal expenditure level in any way would reduce the firm's returns. But the reduction would be much less severe if it cut both budgets. We estimate that for every $1 underinvested in the relationship, optimal long-term customer profitability would be reduced by $1.25. But if the pharmaceutical company were to make the 25% cut in acquisition investment, every $1 underinvested in the relationship would reduce the customer's optimal long-term profitability by $3.03.

We find a similar result with budget increases. Say the firm increases its total budget beyond the optimal level

by raising both the acquisition and retention budgets by
5%. Under this scenario, every dollar overinvested in the
relationship reduces the long-term customer profitability
from its optimal level by $1.22. But suppose the 5% total
increase were accomplished by increasing the acquisition budget 25%. This is worse because then for every
dollar overinvested in the relationship, the customer's
long-term profitability drops by $2.83.

In fact, finding the optimal balance between investments in acquisition and retention can be more important than finding the optimum amount to invest overall.
It seems reasonable to suppose, for instance, that reducing the optimal total expenditure by 10% should result in
less attractive ROIs than reducing it by 5%. But we found
that was not necessarily the case. To continue with the
pharmaceutical company, we found that reducing the
total budget by simultaneously reducing its acquisition
budget and its retention budget 10% is better (a loss of
$2 in profits for every dollar saved in costs) than reduc-
ing the total budget 5% by decreasing acquisition spending only (at which point the company loses $3 in profits
for every dollar saved in acquisition costs).

Finally, we took our analysis of the three firms down
to a granular level and looked at the impact of choices
in communication channels on investment effectiveness. We were able to obtain precise recommendations
for the optimal communication strategy. We found, for
example, that average customer profitability would be
maximized if the B2B firm allocated 80% of its communication efforts by volume (that is, the number of communications) to e-mail, 11% to phone contacts, 7% to
Web-based interactions (which in this case are all
customer initiated), and 2% to face-to-face contacts. Of
course, these numbers reflect to some extent the cost

differences between the channels. If an e-mail or Web message costs $1, for instance, then a phone call costs $20, and a face-to-face communication, $200.

We were able to go further than an overall breakdown of communication instances by channel, as we can demonstrate with the B2B example. Given the low cost of e-mail communication, an obvious question for the company is "To what extent should e-mail be used in conjunction with other modes of communication?" Our model was able to tell us that the most efficient way to maximize profitability is to use telephone interactions and e-mail communications *simultaneously* 37% of the time that telephone contacts are employed. We also found that 67% of the time a face-to-face contact is employed, an e-mail should accompany it.

• • •

In business environments where decisions about allocating marketing resources increasingly occur at the individual account level, it is critical for marketers to understand that individuals who are easy to acquire and retain may not be the most profitable customers. Our model incorporates profitability into marketing-mix decisions, revealing both how much companies must spend on direct marketing to maximize profitability and how they should most profitably allocate that spending—not only in terms of acquisition and relationship management efforts but even down to the level of choices between various direct communication channels. Managers need not invest huge amounts in gathering data to implement the model; they can safely rely on the information they already collect. Their resource allocation choices, in turn, will provide a clear set of attainable, profit-linked marketing goals for which managers can be fairly held accountable.

What Drives Profitability?

MANY FACTORS go into determining customer profitability, and, of course, they vary from industry to industry and from company to company. Here are the specific factors we looked at in deriving regression equations for acquisition likelihood, relationship duration, and customer profitability at a pharmaceutical firm. This company has three products, one of which accounts for 90% of its revenues. A doctor is considered to have been acquired if he or she writes a prescription for any of the company's products.

Acquisition Likelihood Equation:

Factors affecting acquisition likelihood include

- acquisition expenses
- number of face-to-face contacts and number of telephone contacts the sales reps make to the doctor's office
- number of doctor-initiated contacts made to the firm inquiring about its products
- doctor's age, gender, and years of experience
- average number of patients the doctor sees per month

Relationship Duration Equation:

Factors affecting the relationship duration include

- retention expenses
- number of face-to-face contacts and number of telephone contacts the sales reps make to the doctor's office
- number of doctor-initiated contacts made to the firm inquiring about its products

- number of prescriptions written for the firm's products
- number of different drugs for which prescriptions are written
- share of prescriptions (of the total number of prescriptions written, how many were for the firm)

Profitability Equation:

Factors affecting profitability include

- acquisition expenses
- retention expenses
- number of face-to-face contacts and number of telephone contacts the sales reps make to the doctor's office
- number of doctor-initiated contacts made to the firm inquiring about its products
- number of prescriptions written for the firm's products
- number of different drugs for which prescriptions are written
- share of prescriptions
- estimated relationship duration

Notes

1. Werner Reinartz, Jacquelyn Thomas, and V. Kumar, "Balancing Acquisition and Retention Resources to Maximize Customer Profitability," Insead working paper no. 2004/28/MKT (2004).

Originally published in July–August 2004
Reprint R0407

How CEOs Manage
Growth Agendas

KENNETH W. FREEMAN, GEORGE NOLEN,

JOHN TYSON, KENNETH D. LEWIS, AND

ROBERT GREIFELD, WITH AN

INTRODUCTION BY RANJAY GULATI

Executive Summary

WHEN DOES IT MAKE SENSE for companies to grow from within? When is it better to gain new capabilities or access to markets by merging with or acquiring other companies? When should you sacrifice the bottom line in order to nurture the top line?

In a thought-provoking series of essays, five executives—Kenneth Freeman of Quest Diagnostics, George Nolen of Siemens USA, John Tyson of Tyson Foods, Kenneth Lewis of Bank of America, and Robert Greifeld of Nasdaq—describe how they have approached top-line growth in various leadership roles throughout their careers. They write candidly about their struggles and successes along the way, relaying growth strategies as diverse as the companies and industries they represent.

The leaders' different tactics have almost everything to do with their companies' particular strengths, weaknesses, and needs. Freeman, for instance, emphasizes the importance of knowing when to put on the brakes. When he first became CEO of Quest, he froze acquisitions for a few years so the company could focus on internal processes and "earn the right to grow." But for Greifeld, it's all about innovation, which "shakes up competitive stasis and propels even mature businesses forward."

The executives agree, though, that companies can grow (and can do so profitably) by distinguishing their offerings from those of other organizations. As Ranjay Gulati of Northwestern's Kellogg School of Management points out in his introduction to the essays, no matter what strategies are in play, "it's important to remember that growth comes in many forms and takes patience. . . . The key is to be ready to act on whatever types of opportunities arise."

Businesspeople across a wide range of industries have increasingly begun to identify maturation and commoditization as emerging challenges. Whether because of globalization, maturing technologies, ease of imitation, decreasing barriers to entry, open standards in technology markets, or pressures from customers who are themselves being squeezed, more and more companies are feeling the intensity of price competition, leading many to describe their businesses as commodity markets. It's one thing if you have an inherent cost advantage, like Dell or Wal-Mart. But most companies don't, and for them, commoditization is a deadly game. When you're constantly scrambling to make your margins, you have to strain to think about the top line.

Everyone wants to find ways to grow, but real power lies in doing so profitably—and that takes serious work.

This is a theme common to the essays that follow. Five years ago, everyone talked about top-line growth; then the focus became tightening the belt; and now it's back to growth—but this time with profitability. Executives are raising the bar on themselves, which is a good thing. To meet their goals, however, they must find ways to distinguish their offerings. The authors of these essays discuss three interrelated approaches to differentiation: innovation, deepening of customer relationships, and bundling of products and services.

Innovation has long been the primary basis of advantage. Indeed, if you have a unique, first-mover product or service, you can get far ahead of the competition. Every one of the essays in this collection points to the need for innovation. John Tyson, CEO of Tyson Foods, discusses his company's expanding line of protein products, for example, and Quest Diagnostic's Kenneth Freeman is going as far as handing over the CEO title to a scientist who can drive the company toward invention and organic growth. Robert Greifeld, Nasdaq's CEO, tells us that the most dramatic top-line growth opportunities come from finding new ways to make, do, or sell.

But it's getting harder to stand out through product innovation alone—and the advantages, when they occur, are becoming more ephemeral—so we come to the second differentiation tactic: sharpening organizational focus on customers. This approach can help a company distinguish itself in a number of ways, from creating new products or services for specific customer segments to personalizing service. A shift in emphasis from products to customers can be challenging, as it might entail fundamental changes in a company's structure, processes, and, ultimately, culture. Nonetheless, even industries that have relied primarily on product innovation are discovering the importance of gearing their organizational processes more directly to the needs of end customers. For instance, although the pharmaceutical industry has traditionally been driven by the development of unique drugs, marketed primarily to physicians, companies such as Eli Lilly and Pfizer have begun investing heavily in consumer outreach. Becoming more customer oriented is in vogue in other industries as well. Bank of America CEO Kenneth Lewis highlights how he focused his company's operations on quality to lift customer satisfaction scores. Freeman describes hospitals as a long-underserved customer segment; he says that Quest Diagnostics grew quickly once it started treating them as a distinct market. And George Nolen, CEO of Siemens USA, explains how the needs of telecommunications clients are driving innovation.

Stemming from this greater focus on consumers, the third approach to differentiation is to blend products and services, thus providing "solutions" to concrete customer needs. In some organizations, the concept of solutions is little more than a marketing ploy. Yet companies such as IBM—which has combined its hardware, software, and consulting services—have found bundling complementary offerings into a solution to be an effective way to stand out from the crowd. By providing value that is more than the sum of its parts, an integrated offering can deflect the price pressure that arises when you compete with others on product or service attributes alone. While initiatives to provide solutions are gaining popularity in a range of industries, the organizational adjustments required can be monumental. Many companies are stumped by the inability of their internal units to coordinate tasks among themselves, as well as with external suppliers, to deliver customer solutions. Nonetheless, executives see no other way to compete in commoditizing markets. Tyson hints at this in his discussion of developing value-added poultry, beef, and pork: By cooking or flavoring many of its products, the company is moving away from the commodity meat business.

For any of these differentiation vehicles—as the essays in this collection make clear—execution is critical. In many companies, unfortunately, "innovation," "customer focus," and "solutions" are rhetorical claims lacking substance. But organizations that have moved from rhetoric to action have found that delivering on these claims can be quite a stretch. If your company is organized by product, for example, how do you reorient employees to think more broadly about customer needs? How do you train a sales force that's accustomed to selling transactions to sell bundled products and services? Lewis talks about realigning incentives to encourage cross selling, while Tyson addresses the challenge of face-to-face interaction with the customer.

Finally, it's important to remember that growth comes in many forms and takes patience; it is episodic in nature. You may make a big jump forward through an acquisition and then grow slowly and steadily through internal innovations or alliances. The key is to be ready to act on whatever types of opportunities arise.

Kenneth W. Freeman

Chairman of the Board, Quest Diagnostics

My education in growth began with a negative experience. More than 30 years ago, I worked as a financial analyst in the part of Corning that made glass for color televisions—the richest division in the company at the time. We had a tried-and-trusted strategy for boosting revenue: raising prices every year. And the division's largest customer, RCA, threatened every year to build its own glass factory. Eventually, RCA stopped threatening and just did it. In response, Corning was forced to adopt a variable pricing policy that quickly reduced its profits from strong to nonexistent.

Around 20 years later, I had another lesson in the wrong way to grow—this time from Corning Clinical Laboratories (which, along with Corning Nichols Institute, was spun off in 1996 as a separate company, Quest Diagnostics). As the new CEO of Corning Clinical Laboratories, starting in May 1995—and later, as the CEO of Quest Diagnostics—I was expected to turn around an organization that had grown rapidly through acquisition. It had devoured roughly 300 independent testing laboratories over a 13-year period. Immediately before my arrival on the scene, the business had done three major deals and was ramming through integration to get to "synergy" as soon as possible. At the same time, the entire industry had major compliance problems with Medicare. Business fled as our service and our reputation suffered. The government, customers, and employees vied over who disliked our company most. We were unprofitable and going nowhere fast.

As I saw it, we had to earn the right to grow. So I froze acquisitions and kept them frozen for three years, from mid-1995 to mid-1998, while we concentrated on building discipline into our processes. We engaged every employee in the turnaround, first establishing a set of core values and clear, consistent goals for everyone. We also created ground rules and best practices for integrating acquisitions. These guidelines were based on rigorous metrics for customer retention and employee satisfaction, as well as ambitious financial targets. Finally, we walked away from a number of our existing customers—most notably, our largest customer—because we weren't willing to engage in the destructive cycle of price competition that was then rampant in our industry. In essence, before we could grow, we had to shrink.

By 1998, Quest Diagnostics became profitable (barely) and started looking for new acquisition opportunities. We continued the old strategy of geographic expansion, which made the most sense in our industry. (Testing facilities must be reasonably close to doctors' offices and hospitals to quickly turn around lab work.) But we moved more deliberately than we had in the past, acquiring fewer businesses and expending far more effort on those we did buy. We were assuming fewer risks while preparing culturally and organizationally to take a huge step forward.

I don't believe in big deals for their own sake. But when there is an opportunity to change an industry, you have to seize it. SmithKline Beecham Clinical Laboratories (SBCL) presented such an opportunity for Quest Diagnostics. With revenues of $1.6 billion, SBCL was slightly larger than we were and far, far larger than any company we had ever pursued. Indeed, this acquisition—if consummated—would be the largest ever in the medical-testing world and would transform the industry by creating, for the first time, a clear market leader. (The industry is highly fragmented, comprising about 4,500 independent lab companies, most of which do no more than $5 million a year in revenues, as well as thousands of labs in hospitals and physicians' offices.)

To get ready after our long freeze, I wanted to make sure we had the integration process down pat. As a sort of practice run, we acquired a midsize lab in Connecticut. The integration went well, so in August 1999, we acquired SBCL. Once again, I called a moratorium on acquisitions until digestion was essentially complete—that is, until employees and customers gave us positive feedback and we'd accomplished the heavy lifting inherent to the acquisition, such as consolidation of facilities and changes to information systems. The whole process took about two years. In the past, major acquisitions had routinely pushed down our revenues by 10% or more. Because of our new processes and the attention we paid to each customer and employee, our organic revenue growth during the assimilation kept pace with the industry, at 4% to 5% per year.

Since then, although we have continued to match—and in some years beat—the industry's growth rates, we haven't consistently exceeded them, which I view as a disappointment. An important reason, I think, is that while we have fine-tuned our geographic-expansion skills, we have focused too little on market segments, particularly the hospital market. Hospitals have different needs from those of physicians—by far our biggest customer segment—in part because their patients are usually so much sicker. For example, hospitals often require faster turnaround times, a more-specialized menu of tests, a higher degree of responsiveness, and answers to more-technical questions. It's only recently that we've created a separate sales force for hospitals and begun dedicating labs to that segment. There's little doubt that had we treated hospitals as a distinct market all along, we would have grown more rapidly.

Since 1998, we have more than tripled our revenues, from $1.5 billion to $4.7 billion. More than half of that, $2.6 billion, came from M&A; organic growth accounted for only $0.6 billion. We still selectively acquire on the basis of geographic location, but we see enormous new opportunities to accelerate organic growth in areas like genomics and a number of esoteric tests that are currently ordered infrequently but whose use is growing quickly. Organic, of course, doesn't necessarily mean homegrown: We are now getting many of our new product offerings from large and small companies on the outside. These relationships and joint ventures will play as important a role as R&D in our future growth.

Different growth strategies require different kinds of leaders. Over the past nine years, ours was a turnaround—and then a roll up—kind of company, with process discipline and geographic expansion driving growth. In retrospect, I can say that I brought the right talents to the job of CEO. I had led a number of turnarounds, and I'd gained the financial and leadership skills I needed to execute a successful acquisition strategy, whether we sold lab tests or jelly beans.

Today, Quest Diagnostics is a health care company prepared to grow organically through new offerings in medical science and technology. My succession-planning effort sought the person who could best capitalize on our rapidly evolving business model. I've recently passed the CEO baton to our former COO of five years, Surya Mohapatra, who holds a PhD in medical physics and has more than 25 years of experience in the health care industry, including diagnostic imaging.

George Nolen

President and CEO, Siemens USA

Acquisitions have been an extremely important source of top-line growth for Siemens, enabling us to expand quickly into major electronics markets like the United

States. When we've integrated those acquisitions into a solid strategic platform, they have worked well; when we've tried to simply buy our way into the market, they have failed. For example, back in the late 1980s, we bought a large U.S.-based distributor of telephone systems, hoping to sell products that Siemens manufactured in other parts of the world to customers in the United States. But the acquired company was a distributor, not an innovator—and the people developing the products at Siemens didn't understand the needs of U.S. customers—so we were not able to gain any traction in the market, and the business languished. We then opened a manufacturing facility in the United States and established a much better market position. Today, with 65,000 employees in North America, Siemens dedicates more than $700 million and 6,500 employees to R&D in the United States alone. The company's net U.S. income suffered a loss of $553 million in 2001; by 2003, however, the U.S. operations earned a profit of $561 million.

When you have both solid market knowledge and the right distribution channels, acquisitions are often the best way to break into a new geographic location. In the late 1990s, we spent around $8 billion on acquisitions over about four and a half years, in most cases to establish a local presence. Westinghouse Power Generation, one of the businesses we bought during that period, is shaping up as an excellent acquisition for Siemens; it positioned us in the NAFTA market just before the U.S. power boom and provided us with a premier American management team. I don't believe you can be successful without the combination of strong local presence and talent.

Acquisitions have also helped us continue to diversify, which has always been key to our success. In the late 1990s, Siemens was counseled by financial analysts and others to concentrate on telecommunications and information technology, and to get out of transportation, health care, and power generation. Other diversified companies did just that, but we didn't. If you compare the stock progression of those other companies with ours, it's very clear that we made the right decision. I can't say that we knew the power boom was coming, but we have always believed that diversity in our portfolio is a strategic advantage. These days, some are suggesting that we get out of telecommunications—it's a tough business right now. But our customers say they still depend on us. AT&T, for example, is relying on us to build the next generation of optical networks, an initiative of strategic importance to AT&T's future. We know there's going to be some fallout in telecommunications, but our involvement in these next-generation networks around the globe indicates we're well positioned in that market.

Because our portfolio is diverse, we can also look across businesses to find new ways to apply existing technologies. For example, sensor technology that we developed for the automotive industry can also be used in security and health care. And medical imaging has proved to be quite relevant to homeland security. In 2003, the Transportation Security Administration awarded Siemens and Boeing a $1.37 billion joint contract to install and service bomb detection devices for scanning checked baggage in all U.S. commercial airports. We got the work because of our expertise in airport logistics, building security, baggage handling, and X-ray imaging. We were then able to use our knowledge of airports to develop other products and services—information technology, building controls, fire protection, and so forth.

Our success in acquisitions can be attributed in part to our close customer relationships. In April 2004, for instance, Siemens bought DaimlerChrysler's automotive electronics business in Huntsville, Alabama, which immediately boosted our revenue by $1 billion. In addition, the acquisition has expanded our product offerings, enabling us to increase our business with existing customers. DaimlerChrysler's executives didn't want to sell the business to just anyone. They approached us because their company has had a long relationship with Siemens. Furthermore, since most advancements in automotive technology will eventually be derived from electronics, DaimlerChrysler's managers wanted to get the innovation and quality that Siemens could provide.

Of all the factors driving successful growth—a strategic platform, market knowledge, good distribution, a diverse product portfolio, customer relationships—the one that's most critical to success in a mature industry is a progressive attitude toward inventiveness. Companies must consistently find new, more-effective, and creative ways to help both existing and potential customers be more competitive. Whether it's through strategic acquisitions, internal research and development, venture capital investments, or partnerships, business leaders need to see beyond the current way of operating and quickly adapt to fluid market situations. It may be easier to generate that level of change in younger companies operating in growth industries. Nonetheless, for the veterans, nothing can replace the unrelenting pursuit of meaningful innovation.

John Tyson

CEO, Tyson Foods

As businesspeople, we need to accept that top-line growth is a challenge and that it doesn't happen in a linear, constant way. You might grow one quarter, plateau the next, and then maybe shrink as you prune the business so you're ready to grow again.

Tyson is a company that has grown through acquisitions and the dedication of its many team members. We've done 30-plus deals since the mid-1960s—most prominently, the merger with IBP several years ago that virtually doubled our size and brought us into the beef and pork businesses. Integrating the companies was more straightforward than you might think, because everyone wanted to move away from providing commodity meats and toward creating value-added products. The common goal, in other words, was to enhance the meats—to cook them, slice them, or add sauces or flavors, for instance—before selling them. That's going to be a major source of growth for us in the coming years. If you can sell a pound of protein for a dollar instead of 50 cents because you've added convenience or value, you get both top- and bottom-line growth. My father used to say, "Don't do more protein; do more to the protein you have."

At the time of the merger, the old Tyson had been making a shift toward value-added poultry products for maybe ten or 15 years. And over the previous couple of years, IBP had acquired 14 companies that specialized in value-added products. Since those organizations hadn't been integrated into IBP yet, there was really a three-way merger among IBP, its 14 acquisitions, and the old Tyson. All three contributed insights into how to run operations, and we were able to spread and blend that knowledge throughout the newly combined organization. And we had a common foundation: an agriculture-based, operations-focused culture in the business of managing and processing animal products.

M&A doesn't always go so well. In the 1990s, we tried to get into the fish business, but that's different from producing poultry, beef, and pork. We thought regulators might quickly move to quotas based on catch history, but it took them much longer to do so than we'd anticipated. If everyone's competing for the same 100 tons of fish, there are incentives to send boats into rough water and put your fishermen into other dangerous situations, and all of this makes operations difficult. We tried for three or four years and then sold the fish business.

But most of our acquisitions have been successful because of my predecessors' ability to anticipate trends, like the demand for food away from home. Currently, we see our next opportunities for top-line growth coming from three key categories—food service, retail, and international markets.

In food service and retail, our growth will be largely organic in the near future, and a lot of the work will be in tactical execution—on the street, face-to-face, one customer at a time. We need to figure out how to get a poultry consumer to buy beef and pork, and how to extend our existing capabilities. If we can bread or batter chicken, what's to say we can't bread or batter pork and beef? In the IBP acquisition, we got beef and pork luncheon meats, so we'll find ways to add chicken and turkey to that line. We're also dealing with the fact that there are so many different places where people can feed themselves and their families. They can get food just about anywhere—at the ballpark, from a street vendor, or from a machine, for instance. We need to come up with products that fit these delivery systems. In other words, we need to make sure our foods are in front of people any time they decide they're hungry. Wherever you look, you can see a snack or beverage. Can you see a protein product? Probably not—at least not now.

Since Tyson's international operations aren't yet fully developed, our international growth will mostly come from a combination of joint ventures and acquisitions. One way we can enhance our capabilities with local knowledge in various places outside the United States is to get involved in animal production, working with countries (such as Brazil, China, and Russia) that have the large-scale agricultural capacity to yield grain for feed. Another possible approach follows a marketing model: We can get in at the back end of the production system, buying raw material that's already processed— the cuts we need in order to make value-added products. The strategy we choose will depend to some extent on agricultural trade policy.

Whether a company is growing organically or through acquisition, three factors are critical to its success. The first is a knack for anticipating trends, as I have mentioned. The second is the ability to act and react quickly. If you get a call from somebody who's ready to sell, you need to be able to move fast—within a week—if you're interested. Otherwise, it'll be too late; you'll miss out on the deal. (I've seen this happen many times.) If you're not interested, you should tell the seller right away, so you don't damage the relationship. And that brings us to the third factor: connections with others in the industry. Protein is still largely a family business, and there's not a lot of turnover; you see the same people, spanning several generations, when you go to industry and trade shows year after year. If you make a practice of establishing and maintaining solid relationships, you'll have early access to important news—for instance, that a company might soon be for sale—and therefore to critical opportunities.

Kenneth D. Lewis

CEO, Bank of America

Bank of America has been in the news lately as a result of its acquiring FleetBoston Financial. After roughly two decades of growth through acquisitions made by my predecessor, Hugh McColl, we have spent the past five years emphasizing organic growth. The Fleet deal, however, has prompted a lot of questions about whether we're changing our strategy.

Believe it or not, I really don't see this as a departure. Our decision to focus on organic growth has paid off— we grew more than 10% last year, in a time when it wasn't easy to get revenue. As of early 2001, we were basically running even on net new customer accounts. We're now on pace to gain more than two million of them this year, not including new accounts that came with the merger. And we continue to grow our core business; we'll be building about 500 new branches in the next three to four years. That's a long-term investment in top-line growth, because it takes about 18 months to realize gains from a new branch.

But the reality is, at some point you have to be opportunistic. Why Fleet, and why now? It was available. We looked at it as you might look at the last piece of attractive beachfront property. There's a tremendous base of wealth in New England, and acquiring Fleet will broaden our opportunity to achieve long-term organic growth. Furthermore, Bank of America's focus on holistic cus-

tomer relationships will help us connect with many of
Fleet's customers; we can recommend financial solutions
that fit their needs.

In integrating the companies, we'll apply lessons from
past mergers. We learned a lot when we merged with
Barnett Banks in 1998, back when we were NationsBank.
The major problem we had in that merger was that we
tried to do too much at once. Both banks had branches
in Florida, so we got rid of the overlap by closing about
200 branches. At the same time, we were installing a new
transaction-processing system and rebranding the
remaining branches. We did all the work very quickly,
much of it over a single weekend. That was in October
1998; on September 30, 1998, NationsBank and the
old Bank of America had merged, later to become the
new Bank of America. In hindsight, it was a classic example of spreading ourselves too thin. The resulting glitches
in systems and processes caused significant customer
dissatisfaction and runoff.

We also made some miscalculations in our branch
closings. Our business models indicated that people
would go to the bank that was closest to them and most
convenient, but many customers ended up driving right
past a new NationsBank branch, looking for a Barnett
branch because they were familiar with the brand. Ultimately, the merger put us where we are today in terms of
understanding customer needs, so I'm glad we did it. But
the integration process took a toll on our brand, our customer loyalty, our financial results, and our associates.

With Fleet, the degree of difficulty is lower because
we've learned from past experience and there's no
branch overlap. However, we want to avoid focusing the
whole company on this integration. A key message we've

been trying to convey is this: If you're not involved in the merger, don't get involved. We won't succeed if the other 75% of the company doesn't continue with business as usual. A commercial-banking executive in the Midwest doesn't need to come to New England to work on the Fleet merger; he or she needs to focus on making plans. I'll be doing both, though I expect that my participation in the merger will be much heavier early on and will lessen as more people emerge as leaders in their segments.

When we announced our intention to focus on organic growth, five years ago, we knew we'd have to concentrate on three aspects of how we run the company: placing the right people in the right roles, matching our operations to our rhetoric, and emphasizing quality and productivity in every part of the business. These continue to be our top priorities as we move forward with the Fleet merger.

When it comes to people placement, the primary concern is whether you have the right staff for the business you want to pursue. Because Fleet outsourced its home loans, walk-in customers inquiring about mortgages had to call a toll-free number for assistance. We're filling the gap in service by assigning mortgage brokers to each of the old Fleet branches.

As for matching rhetoric to operations, we've improved the connection between strategy and incentives. A few years ago, when we began asking our branch managers to hand off qualified customers to our premier and private bank segments, we didn't offer adequate rewards for compliance. Why would associates turn over their best customers, even for the good of the entire company, if doing so ran counter to their own incentives? We had to provide a financial rationale for branch managers to share those names.

And finally, our focus on quality and productivity is aimed at reducing errors—which is critical to retaining customers and staying profitable. Only customers who give us high satisfaction scores—nines and tens on a one-to-ten scale—are likely to stay with us, buy more products, and recommend our services to other people. To make our processes more efficient, all of our managers have completed individual Green Belt projects. (Green Belt is a certification level in the Six Sigma discipline.) We now have hundreds of process improvement projects in the works at any given time. Since 2001, our payments error rate has gone down 22%, and we have increased payment speed tenfold in the same time frame. And since early 2003, we have reduced our deposit error rate by 83% and increased customer delight—those nine and ten scores—from a baseline of 41% to almost 52%. All of these improvements have contributed to the addition of more than 2.5 million customers during this period.

I expect that our future long-term growth will continue to be largely organic, but we might occasionally complement it with strategic fill-in acquisitions. Companies can always grow the top line by improving relationships with old customers and attracting new ones, but it's necessary to keep sustainability in mind. Our goal at Bank of America is to balance short-term and long-term strategies and tactics. I believe that our willingness and ability to take advantage of an opportunity like acquiring Fleet, as well as our commitment to organic growth in all our businesses, will serve us well in the foreseeable future.

Robert Greifeld

President and CEO, the Nasdaq Stock Market

Companies seeking nonlinear top-line growth must innovate. That lesson has been reinforced repeatedly throughout my career. In the early 1990s at Automated Securities Clearance, when I was CEO there, we were the first company on the market with an electronic order management system for Nasdaq stocks. Our product was unique and provided considerable added value; as a result, we could extract an innovator's profit margin. We also created one of the first electronic communications networks (ECNs), the Brass Utility—a precursor to the Brut ECN, which is still a vigorous competitor in the transactions business. Today I am learning the value of innovation again, only this time my instructors are Nasdaq's listed companies. Those with the most dramatic top-line growth are, almost without exception, the businesses that have discovered a new way to make, do, or sell something.

Innovation creates first movers who reap first-mover profit margins. It shakes up competitive stasis and propels even mature businesses forward, and it is mercifully tolerant of mistakes. For companies focused on organic growth, failure—in reasonable proportion to success—is a sign of health. Mergers and acquisitions, by contrast, must be implemented meticulously, according to an exhaustive plan. M&A is a poor growth strategy for companies harboring even the slightest doubt about their ability to execute.

So innovation, not surprisingly, is the incendiary we are using to ignite growth at Nasdaq itself. A key target for such change is the transaction part of the stock market business, an area that is approaching commoditization. Competition is tough, not only brandwise from the New York Stock Exchange, but also technologically from the ECNs. The past few years have been difficult for us, as they have been for many businesses; we are aggressively competing for market share in an environment that has seen declines in trading volume relative to historic highs, coupled with price compression.

As a stock market, we face certain industry-specific challenges. For instance, we must work within stricter parameters than other organizations. Our corporate charter compels us to put the interests of investors above our own profit, which often means we can't implement innovation as quickly as we'd like. But what's good for investors is good for our market and, ultimately, for our business.

We also, however, have advantages that other types of organizations don't, including access to thousands of innovation leaders. We have gleaned a number of practices from our listed companies. From Terry Semel at Yahoo, we've learned to use teams to generate and then rigorously review new ideas. From H.K. Desai of QLogic, we've adopted the tactic of staging town hall meetings at every company location after every earnings call. Other changes include putting an electronic suggestion box on our intranet, holding regular meetings with all our vice presidents in which each presents a new idea for discussion, and engaging in a very detailed form of analysis that measures the profitability of each of our products.

Our renewed emphasis on innovation has produced two offerings that we think will boost our top line. First, we've expanded our listings business. Traditionally, companies have chosen between Nasdaq and the NYSE. In January, though, we introduced a dual-listing service, and since then, seven companies representing more than $157 billion in market capitalization have elected to list on both exchanges. Second, to compete aggressively with NYSE and others, we are putting in place a new sales team to win exclusive listings.

In addition, we have developed the Closing Cross, a new type of order facility that will provide investors with more transparency and price discovery at the market close at 4:00 PM. The Closing Cross brings together buy and sell interests in specific stocks and executes all shares for each stock at a single price, one that reflects the true supply and demand for Nasdaq securities. An increase in transparency and accuracy gives the industry greater certainty in pricing major transactions, as well as making it possible to more accurately set net asset values for mutual funds. And it fuels our business growth by providing revenue on both sides of the transaction at the close.

Nasdaq has one of the most recognizable indexes in the world, yet our stock market business and our index are not the same thing. We must make sure that our business mirrors the businesses listed on our market. In other words, we can never stop innovating.

Originally published in July–August 2004
Reprint R0407K

Value Innovation

The Strategic Logic of High Growth

W. CHAN KIM AND RENÉE MAUBORGNE

Executive Summary

WHY ARE SOME COMPANIES able to sustain high growth while others are not? To answer that question, Insead professors W. Chan Kim and Renée Mauborgne spent five years studying more than 30 companies around the world. They found that the thinking of less successful organizations is often dominated by the idea of staying ahead of the competition. In stark contrast, high-growth companies pay little attention to matching or beating their rivals. Instead, they seek to make their competitors irrelevant through what the authors call "value innovation."

Conventional strategic logic and value innovation differ along the basic dimensions of strategy. Many companies take their industry's conditions as given; value innovators don't. While many organizations let their rivals set the parameters of their strategic thinking, value innovators do not use competitors as benchmarks. Rather than focus on differences between customers, value innovators look for things that customers value in common. Instead of viewing opportunities through a lens of existing assets and capabilities, value innovators ask, What if we start anew?

In this classic HBR article, first published in 1997, the authors tell the story of the French hotelier Accor, which discarded the notion of what a hotel is supposed to look like in the interest of delivering what customers really want: a good night's sleep at a low price. And Virgin Atlantic challenged airline industry conventions by eliminating first-class service and channeling savings into innovations for business-class passengers. Those companies didn't set out to build advantages over the competition, but in the end, their innovative practices led them to do just that.

Most companies focus on matching and beating their rivals. As a result, their strategies tend to take on similar dimensions. What ensues is head-to-head competition based largely on incremental improvements in cost, quality, or both. W. Chan Kim and Renée Mauborgne from Insead study how innovative companies break free from the pack by staking out fundamentally new market space—that is, by creating products or services for which there are no direct competitors. This path to value innovation requires a different competitive mind-set and a systematic way of looking for opportunities. Instead of searching within the conventional boundaries of industry competition, managers can look methodically across those boundaries to find unoccupied territory that represents real value innovation. The French hotel chain Accor, for example, discarded conventional notions of what a budget hotel should be and offered what most value-conscious customers really wanted: a good night's sleep at a low price.

During the past decade, the authors have developed the idea of value innovation, often in the pages of HBR. This article presents the notion in its original, most fundamental form.

After a decade of downsizing and increasingly intense competition, profitable growth is a tremendous challenge many companies face. Why do some companies achieve sustained high growth in both revenues and profits? In a five-year study of high-growth companies and their less successful competitors, we found that the answer lay in the way each group approached strategy. The difference in approach was not a matter of managers choosing one analytical tool or planning model over another. The difference was in the companies' fundamental, implicit assumptions about strategy. The less successful companies took a conventional approach: Their strategic thinking was dominated by the idea of staying ahead of the competition. In stark contrast, the high-growth companies paid little attention to matching or beating their rivals. Instead, they sought to make their competitors irrelevant through a strategic logic we call value innovation.

Consider Bert Claeys, a Belgian company that operates movie theaters. From the 1960s to the 1980s, the movie theater industry in Belgium was declining steadily. With the spread of videocassette recorders and satellite and cable television, the average Belgian's moviegoing dropped from eight to two times per year. By the 1980s, many cinema operators (COs) were forced to shut down.

The COs that remained in business found themselves competing head-to-head for a shrinking market. All took similar actions. They turned cinemas into multiplexes with as many as ten screens, broadened their film offerings to attract all customer segments, expanded their food and drink services, and increased showing times.

Those attempts to leverage existing assets became irrelevant in 1988, when Bert Claeys created Kinepolis. Neither an ordinary cinema nor a multiplex, Kinepolis is the world's first megaplex, with 25 screens and 7,600 seats. By offering moviegoers a radically superior experience, Kinepolis won 50% of the market in Brussels in its first year and expanded the market by about 40%. Today, many Belgians refer not to a night at the movies but to an evening at Kinepolis.

Consider the differences between Kinepolis and other Belgian movie theaters. The typical Belgian multiplex has small viewing rooms that often have no more than 100 seats, screens that measure seven meters by five meters, and 35-millimeter projection equipment. Viewing rooms at Kinepolis have up to 700 seats, and there is so much legroom that viewers do not have to move when someone passes by. Bert Claeys installed oversized seats with individual armrests and designed a steep slope in the floor to ensure everyone an unobstructed view. At Kinepolis, screens measure up to 29 meters by ten meters and rest on their own foundations so that sound vibrations are not transmitted among screens. Many viewing rooms have 70-millimeter projection equipment and state-of-the-art sound equipment. And Bert Claeys challenged the industry's conventional wisdom about the importance of prime, city-center real estate by locating Kinepolis off the ring road circling Brussels, 15 minutes from downtown. Patrons park for free in large, well-lit lots. (The company was prepared to lose out on foot traffic in order to solve a major problem for the majority of moviegoers in Brussels: the scarcity and high cost of parking.)

Bert Claeys can offer this radically superior cinema experience without increasing ticket prices because the concept of the megaplex results in one of the lowest cost structures in the industry. The average cost to build a seat at Kinepolis is about 70,000 Belgian francs, less than half the industry's average in Brussels. Why? The megaplex's location outside the city is cheaper; its size gives it economies in purchasing, more leverage with film distributors, and better overall margins; and with 25 screens served by a central ticketing and lobby area, Kinepolis achieves economies in personnel and over-head. Furthermore, the company spends very little on advertising because its value innovation generates a lot of word-of-mouth praise.

Within its supposedly unattractive industry, Kinepolis has achieved spectacular growth and profits. Belgian moviegoers now attend the cinema more frequently because of Kinepolis, and people who never went to the movies have been drawn into the market. Instead of battling competitors over targeted segments of the market, Bert Claeys made the competition irrelevant. (See the exhibit "How Kinepolis Achieves Profitable Growth.")

Why did other Belgian COs fail to seize that opportunity? Like the others, Bert Claeys was an incumbent with sunk investments: a network of cinemas across Belgium. In fact, Kinepolis would have represented a smaller investment for some COs than it did for Bert Claeys. Most COs were thinking—implicitly or explicitly—along these lines: The industry is shrinking, so we should not make major investments—especially in fixed assets. But we can improve our performance by outdoing our rivals on each of the key dimensions of competition. We must have better films, better services, and better marketing.

Bert Claeys followed a different strategic logic. The company set out to make its cinema experience not better than that at competitors' theaters but completely different—and irresistible. The company thought as if it were a new entrant into the market. It sought to reach the mass of moviegoers by focusing on widely shared needs. In order to give most moviegoers a package they would value highly, the company put aside conventional thinking about what a theater is supposed to look like.

How Kinepolis Achieves Profitable Growth

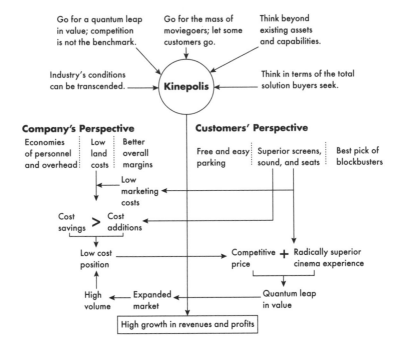

And it did that while reducing its costs. That's the logic behind value innovation.

Conventional Logic Versus Value Innovation

Conventional strategic logic and the logic of value innovation differ along the five basic dimensions of strategy. Those differences determine which questions managers ask, what opportunities they see and pursue, and how they understand risk. (See the exhibit "Two Strategic Logics.")

INDUSTRY ASSUMPTIONS

Many companies take their industries' conditions as given and set strategy accordingly. Value innovators don't. No matter how the rest of the industry is faring, value innovators look for blockbuster ideas and quantum leaps in value. Had Bert Claeys, for example, taken its industry's conditions as given, it would never have created a megaplex. The company would have followed the endgame strategy of milking its business or the zero-sum strategy of competing for share in a shrinking market. Instead, through Kinepolis, the company transcended the industry's conditions.

STRATEGIC FOCUS

Many organizations let competitors set the parameters of their strategic thinking. They compare their strengths and weaknesses with those of their rivals and focus on building advantages. Consider this example. For years, the major U.S. television networks used the same format for news programming. All aired shows in the same time slot and competed on their analysis of events, the professionalism with which they delivered the news, and the

Two Strategic Logics

The Five Dimensions of Strategy	Conventional Logic	Value Innovation Logic
Industry Assumptions	Industry's conditions are given.	Industry's conditions can be shaped.
Strategic Focus	A company should build competitive advantages. The aim is to beat the competition.	Competition is not the benchmark. A company should pursue a quantum leap in value to dominate the market.
Customers	A company should retain and expand its customer base through further segmentation and customization. It should focus on the differences in what customers value.	A value innovator targets the mass of buyers and willingly lets some existing customers go. It focuses on the key commonalities in what customers value.
Assets and Capabilities	A company should leverage its existing assets and capabilities.	A company must not be constrained by what it already has. It must ask, What would we do if we were starting anew?
Product and Service Offerings	An industry's traditional boundaries determine the products and services a company offers. The goal is to maximize the value of those offerings.	A value innovator thinks in terms of the total solution customers seek, even if that takes the company beyond its industry's traditional offerings.

popularity of their anchors. In 1980, CNN came on the scene with a focus on creating a quantum leap in value, not on competing with the networks. CNN replaced the networks' format with real-time news from around the world, 24 hours a day. CNN not only emerged as the leader in global news broadcasting—and created new demand around the globe—but also was able to produce 24 hours of real-time news for one-fifth the cost of one hour of network news.

Conventional logic leads companies to compete at the margin for incremental share. The logic of value innovation starts with an ambition to dominate the market by offering a tremendous leap in value. Value innovators never say, Here's what competitors are doing; let's do this in response. They monitor competitors but do not use them as benchmarks. Hasso Plattner, vice chairman of SAP, the global leader in business application software, puts it this way: "I'm not interested in whether we are better than the competition. The real test is, will most buyers still seek out our products even if we don't market them?"

Because value innovators don't focus on competing, they can distinguish the factors that deliver superior value from all the factors the industry competes on. They do not expend their resources to offer certain product and service features just because that is what their rivals are doing. CNN, for example, decided not to compete with the networks in the race to get big-name anchors. Companies that follow the logic of value innovation free up their resources to identify and deliver completely new sources of value. Ironically, even though value innovators do not set out to build advantages over the competition, they often end up achieving the greatest competitive advantages.

CUSTOMERS

Many companies seek growth through retaining and expanding their customer bases. This often leads to finer segmentation and greater customization of offerings to meet specialized needs. Value innovation follows a different logic. Instead of focusing on the differences between customers, value innovators build on the powerful commonalities in the features that customers value. In the words of a senior executive at the French hotelier Accor, "We focus on what unites customers. Customers' differences often prevent you from seeing what's most important." Value innovators believe that most people will put their differences aside if they are offered a considerable increase in value. Those companies shoot for the core of the market, even if it means losing some of their customers.

ASSETS AND CAPABILITIES

Many companies view business opportunities through the lens of their existing assets and capabilities. They ask, Given what we have, what is the best we can do? In contrast, value innovators ask, What if we start anew? That is the question the British company Virgin Group put to itself in the late 1980s. The company had a sizable chain of small music stores across the United Kingdom when it came up with the idea of music and entertainment megastores, which would offer customers a tremendous leap in value. Seeing that its small stores could not be leveraged to seize that opportunity, the company decided to sell off the entire chain. As one of Virgin's executives puts it, "We don't let what we can do today condition our view of what it takes to win tomorrow. We take a clean slate approach."

This is not to say that value innovators never leverage their existing assets and capabilities; they often do. But, more important, they assess business opportunities without being biased or constrained by where they are at a given moment. For that reason, value innovators not only have more insight into where value for buyers resides—and how it is changing—but also are much more likely to act on that insight.

PRODUCT AND SERVICE OFFERINGS

Conventional competition takes place within clearly established boundaries defined by the products and services the industry traditionally offers. Value innovators often cross those boundaries. They think in terms of the total solution buyers seek, and they try to overcome the chief compromises their industry forces customers to make—as Bert Claeys did by providing free parking. A senior executive at Compaq Computer describes the approach: "We continually ask where our products and services fit in the total chain of buyers' solutions. We seek to solve buyers' major problems across the entire chain, even if that takes us into a new business. We are not limited by the industry's definition of what we should and should not do."

Creating a New Value Curve

How does the logic of value innovation translate into a company's offerings in the marketplace? Consider the case of Accor. In the mid-1980s, the budget hotel industry in France was suffering from stagnation and overcapacity. Accor's cochairmen, Paul Dubrule and Gérard Pélisson, challenged the company's managers to create a major leap in value for customers. The managers were urged to forget everything they knew about the existing rules, practices, and traditions of the industry. They were asked what they would do if Accor were starting fresh.

In 1985, when Accor launched Formule 1, a line of budget hotels, there were two distinct market segments in the industry. One segment consisted of no-star and one-star hotels, whose average price per room was between 60 and 90 French francs. Customers came to those hotels just for the low price. The other segment was two-star hotels, with an average price of 200 Fr per room. Those more expensive hotels attracted customers by offering a better sleeping environment than the no-star and one-star hotels. People had come to expect that they would get what they paid for: Either they would pay more and get a decent night's sleep, or they would pay less and put up with poor beds and noise.

Accor's managers began by identifying what customers of all budget hotels—no star, one star, and two star—wanted: a good night's sleep for a low price. Focusing on those widely shared needs, Accor's managers saw an opportunity to overcome the chief compromise that the industry forced customers to make. They asked themselves the following four questions: Which of the factors that our industry takes for granted should be eliminated? Which factors should be reduced well below the industry's standard? Which factors should be raised well above the industry's standard? Which factors should be created that the industry has never offered?

The first question forces managers to consider whether the factors that companies compete on actually deliver value to consumers. Often those factors are taken for granted, even though they have no value or even detract from value. Sometimes what buyers value changes fundamentally, but companies that are focused on benchmarking one another do not act on—or even perceive—the change. The second question forces managers to determine whether products and services have been overdesigned in the race to match and beat the competition. The third question pushes managers to uncover and eliminate the compromises their industry forces customers to make. The fourth question helps managers break out of the industry's established boundaries to discover entirely new sources of value for consumers.

In answering the questions, Accor came up with a new concept for a hotel, which led to the launch of Formule 1. First, the company eliminated such standard hotel features as costly restaurants and appealing lounges. Accor reckoned that even though it might lose some customers, most people would do without those features.

Accor's managers believed that budget hotels were overserving customers along other dimensions as well. On those, Formule 1 offers less than many no-star hotels do. For example, receptionists are on hand only during peak check-in and checkout hours. At all other times, customers use an automated teller. Rooms at a Formule 1 hotel are small and equipped only with a bed and the bare necessities—no stationery, desks, or decorations. Instead of closets and dressers, there are a few shelves and a pole for clothing in one corner of the room. The rooms themselves are modular blocks manufactured in a factory, a method that results in economies of scale in production, high quality control, and good sound insulation.

Formule 1 gives Accor considerable cost advantages. The company cut in half the average cost of building a room, and its staff costs dropped from between 25% and

35% of sales—the industry average—to between 20% and 23%. Those cost savings have allowed Accor to improve the features customers value most to levels beyond those of the average French two-star hotel, but the price is only marginally above that of one-star hotels.

Customers have rewarded Accor for its value innovation. The company has not only captured the mass of French budget hotel customers but also expanded the market. From truck drivers who previously slept in their vehicles to businesspeople needing a few hours of rest, new customers have been drawn to the budget category. Formule 1 made the competition irrelevant. At last count, Formule 1's market share in France was greater than the sum of the five next largest players.

The extent of Accor's departure from the standard thinking of its industry can be seen in what we call a value curve—a graphic depiction of a company's relative performance across its industry's key success factors. (See the exhibit "Formule 1's Value Curve.") According to the conventional logic of competition, an industry's value curve follows one basic shape. Rivals try to improve value by offering a little more for a little less, but most don't challenge the shape of the curve.

Like Accor, all the high-performing companies we studied created fundamentally new and superior value curves. They achieved that through a combination of eliminating features, creating features, and reducing and raising features to levels unprecedented in their industries. Take, for example, SAP, which was started in the early 1970s by five former IBM employees in Walldorf, Germany, and became the worldwide industry leader. Until the 1980s, business application software makers focused on subsegmenting the market and customizing their offerings to meet buyers' functional needs, such as production management, logistics, human resources, and payroll.

While most software companies were focusing on improving the performance of particular application products, SAP took aim at the mass of buyers. Instead of competing on customers' differences, SAP sought out commonalities in what customers value. The company correctly hypothesized that for most customers, the

---

Formule 1's Value Curve

Formule 1 offers unprecedented value to the mass of budget hotel customers in France by giving them much more of what they need most and much less of what they are willing to do without.

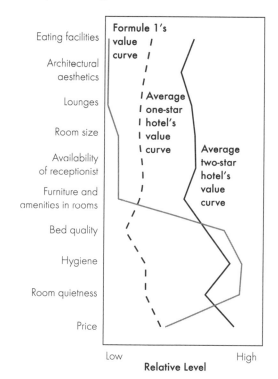

performance advantages of highly customized, individual software modules had been overestimated. Such modules forfeited the efficiency and information advantages of an integrated system, which allows real-time data exchange across a company.

In 1979, SAP launched R/2, a line of real-time, integrated business application software for mainframe computers. R/2 has no restriction on the platform of the host hardware; buyers can capitalize on the best hardware available and reduce their maintenance costs dramatically. Most important, R/2 leads to huge gains in accuracy and efficiency because a company needs to enter its data only once. And R/2 improves the flow of information. A sales manager, for example, can find out when a product will be delivered and why it is late by cross-referencing the production database. SAP's growth and profits have exceeded its industry's. In 1992, SAP achieved a new value innovation with R/3, a line of software for the client-server market.

The Trap of Competing, the Necessity of Repeating

What happens once a company has created a new value curve? Sooner or later, the competition tries to imitate it. In many industries, value innovators do not face a credible challenge for many years, but in others, rivals appear more quickly. Eventually, however, a value innovator will find its growth and profits under attack. Too often, in an attempt to defend its hard-earned customer base, the company launches offenses. But the imitators often persist, and the value innovator—despite its best intentions—may end up in a race to beat the competition.

Obsessed with hanging on to market share, the company may fall into the trap of conventional strategic logic. If the company doesn't find its way out of the trap, the basic shape of its value curve will begin to look just like those of its rivals.

Consider this example. When Compaq Computer launched its first personal computer in 1983, most PC buyers were sophisticated corporate users and technology enthusiasts. IBM had defined the industry's value curve. Compaq's first offering—the first IBM-compatible PC—represented a completely new value curve. Compaq's product not only was technologically superb but also was priced roughly 15% below IBM's. Within three years of its launch, Compaq joined the *Fortune* 500. No other company had ever achieved that status as quickly.

How did IBM respond? It tried to match and beat Compaq's value curve. And Compaq, determined to defend itself, became focused on beating IBM. But while IBM and Compaq were battling over feature enhancements, most buyers were becoming more sensitive to price. User-friendliness was becoming more important to customers than the latest technology. Compaq's focus on competing with IBM led the company to produce a line of PCs that were overengineered and overpriced for most buyers. When IBM walked off the cliff in the late 1980s, Compaq was following close behind.

Could Compaq have foreseen the need to create another value innovation rather than go head-to-head against IBM? If Compaq had monitored the industry's value curves, it would have realized that by the mid- to late 1980s, IBM's and other PC makers' value curves were converging with its own. And by the late 1980s, the curves were nearly identical. That should have been the signal to Compaq that it was time for another quantum leap.

Monitoring value curves may also keep a company from pursuing innovation when there is still a huge profit stream to be collected from its current offering. In some rapidly emerging industries, companies must innovate frequently. In many other industries, companies can harvest their successes for a long time; a radically different value curve is difficult for incumbents to imitate, and the volume advantages that come with value innovation make imitation costly. Kinepolis, Formule 1, and CNN, for example, have enjoyed uncontested dominance for a long time. CNN's value innovation was not challenged for almost ten years. Yet we have seen companies pursue novelty for novelty's sake, driven by internal pressures to leverage unique competencies or to apply the latest technology. Value innovation is about offering unprecedented value, not technology or competencies. It is not the same as being first to market.

When a company's value curve is fundamentally different from that of the rest of the industry—and the difference is valued by most customers—managers should resist innovation. Instead, companies should embark on geographic expansion and operational improvements to achieve maximum economies of scale and market coverage. That approach discourages imitation and allows companies to tap the potential of their current value innovation. Bert Claeys, for example, has been rapidly rolling out and improving its Kinepolis concept with Metropolis, a megaplex in Antwerp, and with megaplexes in many countries in Europe and Asia. And Accor has already built more than 300 Formule 1 hotels across Europe, Africa, and Australia. The company is now targeting Asia.

The Three Platforms

The companies we studied that were most successful at repeating value innovation were those that took advantage of all three platforms on which value innovation can take place: product, service, and delivery. The precise meaning of the three platforms varies across industries and companies, but in general, the product platform is the physical product; the service platform is support such as maintenance, customer service, warranties, and training for distributors and retailers; and the delivery platform includes logistics and the channel used to deliver the product to customers.

Too often, managers trying to create a value innovation focus on the product platform and ignore the other two elements. Over time, that approach is not likely to yield many opportunities for repeated value innovation. As customers and technologies change, each platform presents new possibilities. Just as good farmers rotate their crops, good value innovators rotate their value platforms. (See the sidebar "Virgin Atlantic: Flying in the Face of Conventional Logic" at the end of this article.)

The story of Compaq's server business, which was part of the company's successful comeback, illustrates how the three platforms can be used alternately over time to create new value curves. (See the exhibit "How Has Compaq Stayed on Top of the Server Industry?") In late 1989, Compaq introduced its first server, the System-Pro, which was designed to run five network operating systems—SCO UNIX, OS/2, Vines, NetWare, and DOS—and many application programs. Like the SystemPro, most servers could handle many operating systems and application programs. Compaq observed, however, that the majority of customers used only a small fraction of a server's capacity. After identifying the needs that cut across the mass of users, Compaq decided to build a radically simplified server that would be optimized to run NetWare and file and print only. Launched in 1992, the ProSignia was a value innovation on the product platform. The new server gave buyers twice the SystemPro's file-and-print performance at one-third the price. Compaq achieved that value innovation mainly by reducing general application compatibility—a reduction that translated into much lower manufacturing costs.

As competitors tried to imitate the Pro-Signia and value curves in the industry began to converge, Compaq took another leap, this time from the service platform. Viewing its servers not as stand-alone products but as

How Has Compaq Stayed on Top of the Server Industry?

Relative Level

elements of its customers' total computing needs, Compaq saw that 90% of customers' costs were in servicing networks and only 10% were in the server hardware itself. Yet Compaq, like other companies in the industry, had been focusing on maximizing the price/performance ratio of the server hardware, the least costly element for buyers.

Compaq redeployed its resources to bring out the ProLiant 1000, a server that incorporates two innovative pieces of software. The first, SmartStart, configures server hardware and network information to suit a company's operating system and application programs. It slashes the time it takes a customer to configure a server network and makes installation virtually error free so that servers perform reliably from day one. The second piece of software, Insight Manager, helps customers manage their server networks by, for example, spotting overheating boards or troubled disk drives before they break down.

By innovating on the service platform, Compaq created a superior value curve and expanded its market. Companies lacking expertise in information technology had been skeptical of their ability to configure and manage a network server. SmartStart and Insight Manager helped put those companies at ease. The ProLiant 1000 came out a winner.

As more and more companies acquired servers, Compaq observed that its customers often lacked the space to store the equipment properly. Stuffed into closets or left on the floor with tangled wires, expensive servers were often damaged, were certainly not secure, and were difficult to service.

By focusing on customer value—not on competitors—Compaq saw that it was time for another value innovation on the product platform. The company introduced the ProLiant 1000 rack-mountable server, which allows companies to store servers in a tall, lean cabinet in a central location. The product makes efficient use of space and ensures that machines are protected and are easy to monitor, repair, and enhance. Compaq designed the rack mount to fit both its products and those of other manufacturers, thus attracting even more buyers and discouraging imitation. The company's sales and profits rose again as its new value curve diverged from the industry's.

Compaq is now looking to the delivery platform for a value innovation that will dramatically reduce the lead time between a customer's order and the arrival of the equipment. Lead times have forced customers to forecast their needs—a difficult task—and have often required them to patch together costly solutions while waiting for their orders to be filled. Now that servers are widely used and the demands placed on them are multiplying rapidly, Compaq believes that shorter lead times will provide a quantum leap in value for customers. The company is currently working on a delivery option that will permit its products to be built to customers' specifications and shipped within 48 hours of the order. That value innovation will allow Compaq to reduce its inventory costs and minimize the accumulation of outdated stock.

By achieving value innovations on all three platforms, Compaq has been able to maintain a gap between its value curve and those of other players. Despite the pace of competition in its industry, Compaq's repeated value innovations are allowing the company to remain the number one maker of servers worldwide. Since the company's turnaround, overall sales and profits have almost quadrupled.

Driving a Company for High Growth

One of the most striking findings of our research is that despite the profound impact of a company's strategic logic, that logic is often not articulated. And because it goes unstated and unexamined, a company does not necessarily apply a consistent strategic logic across its businesses.

How can senior executives promote value innovation? First, they must identify and articulate the company's prevailing strategic logic. Then they must challenge it. They must stop and think about the industry's assumptions, the company's strategic focus, and the approaches—to customers, assets and capabilities, and product and service offerings—that are taken as given. Having reframed the company's strategic logic around value innovation, senior executives must ask the four questions that translate that thinking into a new value curve: Which of the factors that our industry takes for granted should be eliminated? Which factors should be reduced well below the industry's standard? Which should be raised well above the industry's standard? Which factors should be created that the industry has never offered? Asking the full set of questions—rather than singling out one or two—is necessary for profitable growth. Value innovation is the simultaneous pursuit of radically superior value for buyers and lower costs for companies.

For managers of diversified corporations, the logic of value innovation can be used to identify the most promising possibilities for growth across a portfolio of businesses. The value innovators we studied all have been pioneers in their industries, not necessarily in developing new technologies but in pushing the value they offer customers to new frontiers. Extending the pioneer metaphor can provide a useful way of talking about the growth potential of current and future businesses.

A company's pioneers are the businesses that offer unprecedented value. They are the most powerful sources of profitable growth. At the other extreme are settlers—businesses with value curves that conform to the basic shape of the industry's. Settlers will not generally contribute much to a company's growth. The potential of migrators lies somewhere in between. Such busi-

Testing the Growth Potential of a Portfolio of Businesses

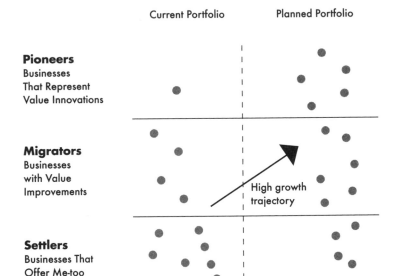

nesses extend the industry's curve by giving customers more for less, but they don't alter its basic shape.

A useful exercise for a management team pursuing growth is to plot the company's current and planned portfolios on a pioneer-migrator-settler map. (See the exhibit "Testing the Growth Potential of a Portfolio of Businesses.") If both the current portfolio and the planned offerings consist mainly of settlers, the company has a low growth trajectory and needs to push for value innovation. The company may well have fallen into the trap of competing. If current and planned offerings consist of a lot of migrators, reasonable growth can be expected. But the company is not exploiting its potential for growth and risks being marginalized by a value innovator. This exercise is especially valuable for managers who want to see beyond today's performance numbers. Revenue, profitability, market share, and customer satisfaction are all measures of a company's current position. Contrary to what conventional strategic thinking suggests, those measures cannot point the way to the future. The pioneer-migrator-settler map can help a company predict and plan future growth and profit, a task that is especially difficult—and crucial—in a fast-changing economy.

Researching the Roots of High Growth

DURING THE PAST FIVE YEARS, we have studied more than 30 companies around the world in approximately 30 industries. We looked at companies with high growth in both revenues and profits and companies with less successful performance records. In an effort to explain the difference in performance between the two groups of companies, we interviewed hundreds of managers, analysts, and researchers. We built strategic, organizational, and performance profiles. We looked for industry or organizational patterns. And we compared the two groups of companies along dimensions that are often thought to be related to a company's potential for growth. Did private companies grow more quickly than public ones? What was the impact on companies of the overall growth of their industry? Did entrepreneurial start-ups have an edge over established incumbents? Were companies led by creative, young radicals likely to grow faster than those run by older managers?

We found that none of those factors mattered in a systematic way. High growth was achieved by both small and large organizations, by companies in high-tech and low-tech industries, by new entrants and incumbents, by private and public companies, and by companies from various countries.

What did matter—consistently—was the way managers in the two groups of companies thought about strategy. In interviewing the managers, we asked them to describe their strategic moves and the thinking behind them. Thus we came to understand their views on each of the five textbook dimensions of strategy: industry assumptions, strategic focus, customers, assets and capabilities, and product and service offerings. We were struck by what emerged from our content analysis of those interviews. The managers of the high-growth companies—irrespective of their industry—all described what we have come to call the logic of value innovation. The managers of the less successful companies all thought along conventional strategic lines.

Intrigued by that finding, we went on to test whether the managers of the high-growth companies applied their strategic thinking to business initiatives in the market-place. We found that they did.

Furthermore, in studying the business launches of about 100 companies, we were able to quantify the impact of value innovation on a company's growth in both revenues and profits. Although 86% of the launches were line extensions—that is, incremental improvements—they accounted for 62% of total revenues and only 39% of total profits. The remaining 14% of the launches—the true value innovations—generated 38% of total revenues and a whopping 61% of total profits.

Virgin Atlantic: Flying in the Face of Conventional Logic

WHEN VIRGIN ATLANTIC AIRWAYS challenged its industry's conventional logic by eliminating first-class ser-vice in 1984, the airline was simply following the logic of value innovation. Most of the industry's profitable rev-enue came from business class, not first class. And first class was a big cost generator. Virgin spotted an oppor-tunity. The airline decided to channel the cost it would save by cutting first-class service into value innovation for business-class passengers.

First, Virgin introduced large, reclining sleeper seats, raising seat comfort in business class well above the industry's standard. Second, Virgin offered free trans-portation to and from the airport—initially in chauffeured limousines and later in specially designed motorcycles called LimoBikes—to speed business-class passengers through snarled city traffic.

With those innovations, which were on the product and service platforms, Virgin attracted not only a large share of the industry's business-class customers but also some full economy fare and first-class passengers of other airlines. Virgin's value innovation separated the company from the pack for many years, but the competition did not stand still. As the value curves of some other airlines began converging with Virgin's value curve, the company went for another leap in value, this time from the service platform.

Virgin observed that most business-class passengers want to use their time productively before and between flights and that, after long-haul flights, they want to freshen up and change their wrinkled clothes before going to meetings. The airline designed lounges where passengers can take showers, have their clothes pressed, enjoy massages, and use state-of-the-art office equipment. The service allows busy executives to make good use of their time and go directly to meetings without first stopping at their hotels—a tremendous value for customers that generates high volume for Virgin. The airline has one of the highest sales per employee in the industry, and its costs per passenger mile are among the lowest. The economics of value innovation create a positive and reinforcing cycle.

When Virgin first challenged the industry's assumptions, its ideas were met with a great deal of skepticism. After all, conventional wisdom says that in order to grow, a company must embrace more, not fewer, market segments. But Virgin deliberately walked away from the revenue generated by first-class passengers. And it further rejected conventional wisdom by conceiving of its business in terms of customer solutions, even if that took the company well beyond an airline's traditional offerings. Virgin has applied the logic of value innovation not just to the airline industry but also to insurance, music, and entertainment retailing. The company has always done more than leverage its existing assets and capabilities. It has been a consistent value innovator.

Originally published in July–August 2004
Reprint R0407P

About the Contributors

R. TIMOTHY S. BREENE is Accenture's Chief Strategy Officer.

JEFFREY H. DYER is the Horace Pratt Beesley Professor of Global Strategy at the Marriott School at Brigham Young University.

GARY GETZ is a director of Strategos.

RANJAY GULATI is the Michael Ludwig Nemmers Distinguished Professor of Strategy and Organizations at Northwestern's Kellogg School of Management.

GARY HAMEL is a visiting professor at London Business School and the chairman of Strategos.

PAUL HEMP is a senior editor at *Harvard Business Review*.

BRIAN A. JOHNSON is a research analyst at Sanford G. Berstein and a former partner at Accenture.

PRASHANT KALE is an assistant professor of corporate strategy and international business at the University of Michigan Business School.

W. CHAN KIM is the BCG Bruce D. Henderson Chair Professor of International Management at Insead.

v. kumar is the ING Chair Professor at the University of Connecticut's School of Business and executive director of the ING Center for Financial Services.

renée mauborgne is The Insead Distinguished Fellow and a professor of strategy and management.

geoffrey a. moore is a managing director of TCG Advisors, venture partner with Mohr, Davidow Ventures, and author of *Living on the Fault Line.*

paul f. nunes is an executive research fellow at Accenture's Institute for High Performance Business.

werner reinartz is an associate professor at Insead.

harbir singh is the Edward H. Bowman Professor of Management at the University of Pennsylvania's Wharton School.

jacquelyn s. thomas is an associate professor at Northwestern University.

Index